A Twentieth-Century Collision

American Intellectual Culture and Pope John Paul II's Idea of a University

Peter M. Collins

UNIVERSITY PRESS OF AMERICA,® INC.
Lanham • Boulder • New York • Toronto • Plymouth, UK

Copyright © 2010 by
University Press of America,® Inc.
4501 Forbes Boulevard
Suite 200
Lanham, Maryland 20706
UPA Acquisitions Department (301) 459-3366

Estover Road
Plymouth PL6 7PY
United Kingdom

All rights reserved
Printed in the United States of America
British Library Cataloging in Publication Information Available

Library of Congress Control Number: 2009927431
ISBN: 978-0-7618-4627-7 (paperback : alk. paper)
eISBN: 978-0-7618-4628-4

∞™ The paper used in this publication meets the minimum
requirements of American National Standard for Information
Sciences—Permanence of Paper for Printed Library Materials,
ANSI Z39.48—1992

Dedicated to Mary Ann Lee Collins,
my lovely and loving wife,
who always will be Pei Tzu Li,
and who became a Catholic by
the grace of God and her own free will
on January 4th, 2003

Contents

Preface   vii

Acknowledgments   ix

Introduction   xi

1   American Philosophy in the Twentieth Century   1
    A. Preliminary Remarks   1
    B. 1880–1920: The Cultural Revolution   2
    C. 1920–1960: The First Phase   6
    D. 1960–2000: The Second Phase   11
    E. Concluding Remarks   19

2   Teaching Philosophy in a Catholic University
    according to John Paul II   29
    A. The Search for Truth and Meaning   29
    B. The Integration of Knowledge in Teaching and Research   31
    C. The Dialogue between Faith and Reason   32
    D. Academic Freedom   33
    E. The Moral Dimension of Academic Life   34
    F. The Academic Community   37
    G. Human Nature   38

Conclusion   41

Bibliography of Materials Used 45

Index 47

About the Author 51

Preface

One of the most significant and crucial reasons for the recent demise of the influence of philosophy in the United States is the narrowing of its scope. The history of this development in American philosophy is complex and is linked to the (so-called) "Golden Age of American Philosophy," occurring in the late nineteenth and early twentieth centuries. The failure of philosophical idealism to win the minds and hearts of Americans was accompanied, near the beginning of the twentieth century, by the development of the philosophical movements of pragmatism, realism, and naturalism. These schools of thought contributed to the later twentieth-century rise of neo-empiricism, logical positivism, and linguistic analysis, in which matters of "traditional" metaphysics and prescriptive ethics are either relegated to the arena of emotion or doomed to oblivion. The postmodernists have taken Dewey's position "beyond agnosticism" to a new level, something like "beyond rationality." Since genuinely metaphysical and ethical questions (such as Who am I? What is my origin? What is my ultimate destiny? What is really real? What is the difference between good and evil?) are *inevitably* related to living a truly intelligent human life; since these questions can be answered rationally *only* within the realms of religion, theology, and philosophy; and since the modes of inquiry into human existence which are associated with these areas are fading fast from American life—or, at least, from American *public* life—a crisis seems to have developed at the heart of American culture.

American Catholic universities, it is contended here, can render a seriously-needed contribution to combating this cultural crisis. This book is intended to elaborate this thesis, first by means of a brief historical survey of the philosophical scene in the United States during the twentieth century, clarifying the existence and nature of this cultural crisis. Secondly, some general principles and specific recommendations concerning the teaching of philosophy in American Catholic universities will be offered as a potential antidote for this crisis. These principles and suggestions are derived from Pope John Paul II's Apostolic Constitution *Ex Corde Ecclesiae* (1990). The discussion of this document on Catholic higher education is supplemented by principles from his Encyclical Letters *Veritatis splendor* (1993) and *Fides et ratio* (1998). In the conclusion, we confront the question of *how* John Paul II's ideal of a Catholic university addresses today's intellectual and cultural problems associated with twentieth-century mainstream American philosophy.

Acknowledgments

I have been interested in philosophy since September, 1956, when I entered Holy Cross Seminary, La Crosse, Wisconsin, and studied the subject for two years. I have been interested in theology since September, 1958, when I took up residence at Theological College and studied the subject at the Catholic University of America, Washington, D.C., for two years. Therefore, I owe the inception of my interest in the interrelationships between philosophy and theology in no small measure to the Diocese of La Crosse, which sponsored education in philosophy at Holy Cross Seminary at a reduced fee, and education in theology at Catholic University *gratis*. Although I left the seminary in 1960, these four years represent not only a most beneficial education, but the beginning of a career in teaching and research, including thirty-two years at Marquette University, Milwaukee, Wisconsin.

The persons who have assisted me substantially along this journey by way of personal relationship and printed material are too numerous to mention. However, in view of the central subject of this study, they obviously would have to include Pope John Paul II. While it clearly is uncommon to acknowledge popes in this kind of instance, I also would like to mention Pope Benedict XVI as being particularly helpful in my attempting to appreciate the interrelationships between philosophy and theology, faith and reason, truth and freedom as a basis for understanding the circumstances of the world in the twenty-first century. Both John Paul II and Benedict XVI recognize the need for comprehending the *whole* of reality through *discovering* it. In the last analysis, "… we really want to hear a clear, insightful statement of our condition. If it is a pope who can best present the dimensions of what we need to know, we are less than human if, on such a ground, we refuse to consider it" (James V. Schall, S.J., *The Regensburg Lecture*, 2007).

Introduction

A survey of American philosophy in the twentieth century opens the possibility of a myriad of conclusions and recommendations for present directions in American culture. A vital aspect of that culture is higher education, a genuine option within that category being the Catholic liberal arts college or the liberal arts college within the Catholic university. The theme of this book revolves around the contention that the teaching of philosophy in American Catholic universities represents a potentially dynamic source of resistance against certain cultural trends connected with the development of American philosophy in the twentieth century.

The late twentieth-century crisis in American culture based upon the bifurcation of faith and reason, accompanied by a growing indifference to religious faith in American society, is associated here with the history of American philosophy. During the past one hundred years, mainstream American philosophy has been narrowed and secularized. Two stages or levels have been detected in these philosophical developments in the United States during the twentieth century: 1) the development of a scientistic and empiricist spirit evident in pragmatism, realism, and naturalism, arising in opposition to forms of idealism; and 2) the subordination of all first-order questions to the analysis of language. The directions of the overall movement have been from philosophical attention to synoptic world-views toward an exclusive emphasis upon the meanings of given propositions, and from a close bond between theology and philosophy toward a radical separation of them.

The following consequences of these developments are noted within the realm of philosophy: 1) extremely technical language, 2) a lack of relevance to daily human living, 3) a deficiency in social and political leadership, 4) an indifference to history, 5) reductionistic orientations, and 6) a failure to capitalize upon the values of Christianity. Several, if not all, of these features have contributed to a severe diminution of an audience for American philosophy. This assessment is highly selective, but it also is highly representative of the mainstream—not only in philosophy, but also in the intellectual milieu of American higher education.

While the redirection of American philosophy cannot be realized quickly or through the efforts of a single social agency, it does not appear presumptuous to contend that Catholic universities in the United States hold a key to unlocking the grip of widespread indifference to philosophy (and theology). The second chapter of this inquiry is intended to address this assertion by focusing upon principles of Pope John Paul II concerning the ideal of a Catholic university. This brief analysis is centered upon John Paul II's Apostolic Constitution *Ex Corde Ecclesiae* (1990). This document on the Catholic university is appreciated in greater depth through suggested relationships to two of John Paul II's Encyclical Letters, *Veritatis splendor* (1993) and *Fides et ratio* (1998). The central focus of the former is morality, while the latter addresses especially the relationships between faith and reason, and between theology and philosophy.

The selection of specific topics in Chapter Two includes the following: 1) search for truth and meaning, 2) integration of knowledge in teaching and research, 3) dialogue between faith and reason, 4) academic freedom, 5) moral dimension of academic life, 6) academic community, and 7) human nature. While these topics are closely interrelated, the last one permeates directly all of the others. Since John Paul II holds that Jesus Christ, Who is God, is the center of the Catholic university—as well as of Catholicism, in general—theology becomes the heart of the curriculum in this kind of academic institution. However, philosophy also enjoys a featured role because of its natural relationship to all the arts and sciences, especially theology; and because of its place in the heritage of the Roman Catholic Church.

This leaves us with the question of *how* John Paul II's ideal of a Catholic university addresses today's intellectual and cultural problems associated with much of mainstream American philosophy. This issue is considered in the Conclusion, and is not unrelated to the persistent criticism in recent years that American Catholic universities have forfeited their identity—and, thus, their unique contribution to American cultural pluralism. The entire book assumes a structure centered upon the assumption that philosophical questions address the kinds of issues that yield meaning for human living. Many of these questions pertain to religious and theological issues as well. Therefore, it seems clear that these philosophical and theological questions are the kinds of questions which educators must address and strive to answer in order to give direction and substance to the educative process.

Chapter One

American Philosophy in the Twentieth Century

A. PRELIMINARY REMARKS

Although formal philosophy (that typically summarized in history of philosophy textbooks and taught in universities) has a relatively short history in the United States, creative intellectual activity has characterized the country since early colonial times. Two somewhat distinctive characteristics of that activity are its practical orientation and its pluralism. The latter becomes apparent in the widely divergent ideas of Puritanism, Deism, materialism, Unitarianism, Transcendentalism, idealism, realism, pragmatism, naturalism, Marxism, Thomism, phenomenology, Zen Buddhism, existentialism, positivism, analytic philosophy,[1] and postmodernism. The practicality of these intellectual pursuits is referred to by Kurtz as the most characteristic theme of the American tradition: "... *ideas are evaluated pragmatically, and their significance is most frequently determined by reference to their practical contexts, their political, religious, moral or social purposes.*"[2] Although pragmatic philosophy, as such (the only indigenous American philosophy), was not born until the early 1870s through the efforts of Charles Peirce and the Metaphysical Club in Cambridge, and not popularized until after 1900 (especially by William James), a highly practical orientation is evident in the writings of Jonathan Edwards, Benjamin Franklin, Thomas Jefferson, Horace Mann and William Torrey Harris. While Americans generally did not tend to cultivate technical philosophy, abstracted from its contexts of origin and application, prior to 1900, philosophical content certainly was implicit in efforts to resolve actual problems encountered in meeting the demands of government, education and other facets of culture.[3]

Even though foreign (especially European) influence upon the history of American thought has been extensive, foreign ideas have been transformed significantly in American culture.[4] An example of this is found in the transplantation of German idealism. Philosophical idealism appears to have been the first technical, systematic philosophy to gain a foothold in the United States, assuming extraordinary importance in the latter half of the nineteenth century in Ohio and St. Louis, Missouri, and later in Concord, Massachusetts, in association with Transcendentalism.[5] This German element, along with British evolutionary naturalism, became major contributors to the "cultural revolution" between 1880 and 1920. A distinction is made thereafter between two historical phases of philosophical development, demarcated by the year 1960. Some personal observations conclude Part I.

B. 1880–1920: THE CULTURAL REVOLUTION

The concatenation of developments in American philosophy between 1880 and 1920 amounts to a veritable revolution. This philosophical revolution was initiated during the immediate post-Civil War period, highlighted by the publication of Charles Darwin's *Origin of Species* in 1859, and developed as merely one aspect of a revolution permeating American culture. The broader perspective on this era has been characterized in terms of a "watershed": "The decade of the nineties is the watershed of American history. As with all watersheds the topography is blurred, but in the perspective of half a century the grand outlines emerge clearly."[6] More specifically, the "decade of the nineties marked the end of an era; it heralded even more unmistakably the beginning of one."[7] "With the decade of the nineties—or roughly from the mid-eighties to the Spanish War—the new America came in as on flood tide."[8]

What constitutes the substance of these "grand outlines"? What faded away and what appeared?

> On the one side lies an America predominantly agricultural; concerned with domestic problems; conforming, intellectually at least, to the political, economic, and moral principles inherited from the seventeenth and eighteenth centuries—an America still in the making, physically and socially; an America on the whole self-confident, self-contained, self-reliant, and conscious of its unique character and of a unique destiny. On the other side lies the modern America, predominantly urban and industrial; inextricably involved in world economy and politics; troubled with the problems that had long been thought peculiar to the Old World; experiencing profound changes in population, social institutions, economy, and technology; and trying to accommodate its traditional institutions and habits of thought to conditions new and in part alien.[9]

Three general aspects of this watershed of American cultural history are distinguished: 1) material circumstances; 2) new techniques, experiences, and challenges; and 3) religious, philosophical, and other concepts.[10] However, "The most important changes were not, in fact, in the purely material but in the philosophical realm, and time had not yet exhausted, had indeed scarcely discovered their significance."[11] Substantiation of this claim seems to be associated with the novelty of this kind of change in American history and the fundamental character of this dimension of human existence:

> It was not only that Americans had to adjust themselves to changes in economy and society more abrupt and pervasive than ever before. It was rather that *for the first time in their national experience they were confronted with a challenge to their philosophical assumptions.* They were not unaccustomed to profound alterations in their physical surroundings; they were unprepared for the crumbling of their cosmic scheme. They were now to be required not only to articulate their economy to a new technology and adjust their society to new ways of life—that was a familiar task—but to make their politics and morals conform to new scientific and philosophical precepts. Under the impact of these new forces, the note of confidence which had long characterized the American accent gave way to doubt, self-assurance to bewilderment, and resolution to confusion (italics added).[12]

The spirit of the references to philosophy in the last two citations entails religion and is not unrelated to what has been called the "common faith" of pre-twentieth century America: that "certain residue of belief common to all partisan groups and acceptable not only to the loyal Christian but to almost all literate Americans of the time."[13] This so-called "fundamental philosophy" or "ideological matrix" providing the context for all thought and discussion derived from the Christian tradition and the secular movements of the seventeenth and eighteenth centuries, and is said to have been rarely doubted or questioned during much of the nineteenth century in the United States. Its three central articles were dualism, fixity, and atomism. The first is the most distinctively religious of these three articles, and signifies a belief in two orders of reality, the material and the spiritual, the latter open to the further distinction between the natural and the supernatural. The human person is viewed as a being of body and soul who participates in all of these realms. The second postulate (fixity) of this common faith, also linked to religion, consists of an assumption that the world is characterized by unchanging fundamental laws and principles of classification; in this kind of universe, the limitation of variation is coordinate with a strong tendency toward repetition and predictability. Thirdly, atomism refers to the postulate that all beings are ultimately simple in nature, that is, composed of a limited number of unanalyzable units.[14]

This common faith seems somewhat akin to what has been referred to as a "religious faith for the most part Calvinistic,"[15] which Americans are said to have professed unanimously while remaining quite thoroughly indifferent to related practices of daily living. Relevant to the Calvinistic feature of this faith is the manner in which the citizens of the United States abandoned ideas: not by new evidence or arguments, but by means of mere change of sentiment.[16] Whatever the mode of, or reasons for, alterations in this common faith, it did encounter radical and effective opposition on a widespread basis during the "cultural revolution" of the late nineteenth and early twentieth centuries, a revolution with its watershed in the 1890s.

What specific factors contributed most to the disintegration of this American common faith? The publication of Darwin's *Origin of Species* in 1859 was singled out above as a significant factor in initiating this substantial cultural change in the United States. Probably, most intellectual historians point to Darwin, along with Herbert Spencer, as the chief perpetrator of the new ideas beginning to sweep over the country in the latter decades of the nineteenth century.[17] However, according to Bowers' thesis, Hegel, as well as Darwin, contributed immensely to the revolutionary modification of the American religious and philosophic tradition.[18] Whereas Hegel represents German romanticism and Darwin is associated with British empiricism, each agrees more closely with the other than with the historic American ideology; and their influence illustrates "how two radically different ideologies were able to reinforce each other at given points in their impact upon American thought and through common action effectively alter its course and direction."[19]

Although Hegel and Darwin differ drastically in their views upon reason and history, they concur (albeit from different perspectives) in promoting the notions of organicism, process, and the priority of the group over the individual. Not coincidentally for the history of American ideology, these three concepts tended to contradict the historical direction of the American tradition embracing the principles of dualism, fixity, and atomic individualism, prevalent at least until 1860 (at about the time that Hegel and Darwin began to be studied seriously in the United States). According to Hegel, organicism signifies the intimate indissoluble association of every being with every other, or each aspect of reality with all the others. Secondly, he argues that everything real constantly changes, that the only permanency lies in process itself, and that nothing possesses abiding value. Finally, particular institutions and individuals are subordinated to the quest of the cosmic spirit for self-fulfillment by means of self-knowledge and self-expression. Darwin's central thesis supported 1) the concept of the continuity of all forms of life (including the human), and the implication that all reality (including life and mind) are phenomena of physical law; 2) the contention that moral and legal codes represent generalizations of human beings based upon natural instinct and desire; and 3) the emphasis in the social and political realms from the individual to the species.[20]

It is clear that the intertwined and coextensive effects of a Hegelian-Darwinian synthesis tended to directly combat the overwhelmingly religious interpretations of reality proposing a dualism of natural and supernatural, the absolute perfection of a Transcendent Being (related to the permanence of essences and moral law), and the dignity of the individual, created in the image and likeness of God.[21] The early impact of the Hegelian-Darwinian synthesis upon the American mind tended toward easy assimilation due to at least three factors: the stimulus it provided to American intellectual life; a more meaningful and positive view of the Civil War than that provided by the traditional American faith; and the initial use of the new principles to defend conservative interests (for example, *laissez-faire* capitalism).[22] A more carefully reflected and mature appreciation of the unorthodoxy of Hegelianism and Darwinism, however, produced different reactions: a denial that they embodied any measure of truth; an attempt to reconcile certain features of them with traditional beliefs; and an acceptance of their central doctrines as sources for constructing a new social criticism.[23] This last (positive) reaction is obviously associated with the remarks above concerning the tremendous impact of Hegel and Darwin upon American intellectual life.

The new social criticism is evident in the instrumentalism of John Dewey, who was influenced directly by both Hegel and Darwin.[24] According to Dewey, the human person is a strictly natural being, a complex animal among other animals; the individual is largely the product of the social environment; and all truth, including moral principles, is radically relative. The opposition of these assertions to the three dimensions of the American tradition noted earlier, when combined with Dewey's influence upon thinking in the United States in the twentieth century, provides significant insight into the nature of the cultural revolution under consideration.

Shifting from the general intellectual pattern, with an emphasis upon the theological and philosophical dimensions of it, to the more exclusively philosophical scene,[25] there existed a clear dominance of idealism throughout the late nineteenth century in the United States. Apart from the more literary Transcendentalism, "American philosophy in the technical sense, which came into its own only after the War of Secession, derived its inspiration from German idealism."[26] The early idealists, in Ohio and St. Louis, were followers of Hegel, as indicated above. Henry C. Brockmeyer, William Torrey Harris and others represented neo-Hegelian absolute idealism, the prevailing mode. However, other noteworthy nineteenth-century idealists, such as George H. Howison and Borden Parker Bowne, became known as "personalists" among the idealists. The best known American philosopher of idealism was Josiah Royce, a Harvard colleague (and neighbor) of William James.[27]

Despite the prominence of idealism for some years, by the beginning of the twentieth century, "The idealists that remained appeared to be, especially in the light of later developments, an anachronistic residue of things, part of the 'cultural lag.'"[28] Philosophers in the idealistic mold continued their philosophical activities, of course;[29] however, the influence of idealism was opposed and undermined by American philosophical movements known as pragmatism, realism, and naturalism. Although the transitions were not instantaneous (for example, Royce claimed to have been influenced by pragmatism,[30] and James appears affected somehow by idealism—and they clearly influenced one another),[31] the demise of idealism did occur rapidly.[32] Although it is hazardous to associate any particular philosophical movement with specific principles due to the variations of thought among representatives of that movement,[33] and to view any particular movement as exclusive of others, the dangers will be overlooked (carefully!) in an effort to portray first very generally and briefly the primary reactions against idealism in American philosophy in the twentieth century.

C. 1920–1960: THE FIRST PHASE

Philosophical idealism became the obvious object of the attack of twentieth-century spokesmen for the clusters of philosophies known as pragmatism, realism, and naturalism.[34] Most late nineteenth and early twentieth-century idealists likely would have endorsed the following propositions: 1) mind is, in some sense, the most fundamental reality, signifying that all that exists is either mind or dependent upon it; 2) reality is an organic whole in which each being or dimension is logically or internally linked to all else; and 3) value and purpose are more than simply features of the human scene due to their cosmic significance. Furthermore, most idealists of this era were defenders of some form of traditional religion, and those who were not were closely attuned to an outlook of rationalistic theology.[35]

Probably the best known of the opponents of idealism in early twentieth-century America are the pragmatists. While Peirce, the so-called founder of the movement, and William James, its popularizer, and Dewey differed radically on relatively substantial matters, they all contributed to the net effect of this indigenous American movement. This effect contributed to the diminution of the influence of traditional conceptions of metaphysics and, correlatively, to the reconstruction of philosophy along empirical lines. While each of these three thinkers advanced what some would recognize as various forms of metaphysics, they concurred in denouncing notions of Absolute Being or ultimate certainty espoused by the idealists. Their influence also began to be felt in the social sciences, where their views of the importance of the practical consequences of ideas were applicable.[36]

The revolt of the realists against early twentieth-century idealism was led by two schools, the "New Realists" and the "Critical Realists." Prominent among the former were Ralph Barton Perry and William P. Montague, and noteworthy among the latter were George Santayana and Arthur O. Lovejoy. Differing on several important matters, the two groups, nevertheless, agreed fundamentally on some basic epistemological issues: they denied the idealistic contention that physical objects are reducible to "ideas," and that objects of experience exist only when experienced. They asserted, on the other hand, that human knowledge does not affect the object, meaning that the relation between knowing and known is an "external" rather than an "internal" relation.[37]

The third group of American philosophers to oppose idealism during this century is known as naturalists. In a broad sense, naturalism can be predicated of any philosophy characterized by the premise that all phenomena can in principle be explicated by means of natural causes or principles. However, American philosophical naturalism regards the logico-empirical method of science as the only procedure suited to establishing cognitive claims. This means that there is no other kind of method for rationalization, and there is no place for recognition of varying kinds of truth (such as religious, moral, aesthetic, etc.). A scientific method is continuous with the operations of thought employed by human beings in matters of daily living, and it alone is applicable in investigating all facets of life and reality. Although Dewey's thought exemplifies naturalism par excellence, not all naturalists were pragmatists and vice versa. In addition, only some realists were naturalists.[38] At any rate, the philosophical impact of naturalism has borne effects noticeable yet today.

Although a generalization of the above generalizations concerning the development of American philosophy between the Civil War and the 1930s may appear unwarranted, it can be helpful if its limitations are borne in mind. This period, referred to as the "Golden Age of American Philosophy" (featuring the thought of Peirce, James, Royce, Santayana, Dewey and Whitehead) has been characterized in terms of three dominant beliefs: 1) that thinking is primarily an activity in response to a specific situation and is directed to solving one or more problems; 2) that ideas and theories must make a difference in the conduct of persons who claim to hold them and in their environments; and 3) that the world can be civilized through the removal of obstacles by means of knowledge. In this "basically humanistic" outlook, all things derive their value in terms of their contributions to securing the good life.[39]

Bearing in mind the relative uniqueness of the thought of each individual philosopher and that the above stated beliefs are held and explained in varying manners,[40] some overarching tendencies of the American philosophical world of this era are evident. These tendencies pertain not merely to the substance of thought involved, but also to the professionalization of philosophy in institutions of higher education. Professionalization of the field expanded with the college movement during the last three decades of the nineteenth century.[41] By 1890, the "independent man of letters" found only minimal social support, and public attention turned increasingly to persons with university affiliation;[42] by 1930, academic philosophy had "come of age."[43] "Philosophers in the schools became the only philosophers, and affiliation with a university became necessary to all those who wished to spend their lives in contemplation."[44]

Two factors associated with the developing professionalization of philosophy are close to the heart of the philosophical revolution of the period: they concern the increasing specialization within philosophy, and the relationship of the field to the social milieu. The former refers to the narrowing scope of philosophy from a focus upon synoptic problems of life, death, and Ultimate Reality to epistemological and logical questions primarily.[45] This direction explains, generally speaking, the scant interest in religious philosophy by students of philosophy completing their education by approximately 1930.[46] As philosophers became more specialized, and their specialties (especially epistemology and logic) became more technical, their influence upon society and society's influence upon them, steadily and understandably diminished.[47] " . . . after 1918 personal concerns ceased to mold the substance of a man's thought, and the social order was no longer directly relevant to philosophizing."[48] "By 1930 philosophy's successful practitioners were purely professional; they tended to specialize within the technical areas and even those who specialized in the practical ones lectured only to fellow specialists and did not apply their ideas to the real world; all popularization was suspect."[49]

Underlying these revolutionary tendencies in philosophy toward specialization and a divorce from social concerns, attended by the professionalization of the field, is a process of secularization. This is a process of the separation of philosophy from theology and all questions traditionally associated with philosophy of religion. This trend took the form in the United States of scientism (in the broader intellectual picture) and empiricism (a technical philosophical orientation). Both appeared to be linked existentially on the American scene (especially in light of World War I) with pessimism, or, perhaps, more accurately, meaninglessness.[50] For example, the development of the "new" physics, chemistry and biology, according to Commager, "threatened to reduce the whole of human thought and art, all the stirrings of the body and the strivings of the mind and the soul, to insignificance." "Not only was man's place in the earth evanescent, accidental, and meaningless; the earth itself was but a flyspeck in a universe equally without purpose or meaning." "Man from all other creatures here below, was seen to be indistinguishable from matter."[51] The cultural revolution and the new scientistic spirit created the appearance of a universe which was impersonal and indifferent; "Logically it made philosophy itself irrelevant if not absurd."[52]

While scientism was rendering traditionally viable philosophies irrelevant, if not absurd, the formulation of new modes of philosophizing (new to the United States, that is) was picking up steam. The general tenor of pragmatism, realism, and naturalism portrayed by at least some of their representatives was anti-metaphysical and empirical.

> In this development of American philosophy the soil was being prepared for modern Empiricism and Positivism. At the beginning of the Second World War, the new tendencies had become dominant and, in a fundamental sense, a distinct period in American philosophy had drawn to a close. In the past, and despite their divergent points of view, American philosophers in general have shared a deep faith in metaphysics as the very core of philosophy. In contemporary thought this faith no longer dominates. On the contrary, antimetaphysical tendencies now prevail in most philosophical discussions.[53]

While this assessment takes us to near mid-century, it explains the general effect of this philosophical revolution upon American philosophy.

The scientism and empiricism which gained a foothold during the earlier years of the twentieth century in the United States were buttressed by a concomitant erosion of traditional religions. While "in everything but law, America, at the opening of the twentieth century, was a Christian nation,"[54] theological speculation gradually parted company with philosophy and diminished in influence, the clergy became less widely concerned with philosophy and gave moral leadership to the scientists, and the churches themselves tended to retreat from intellectual matters and devote more energy to social and economic activities.[55] "Religion came to be largely a matter of observing certain formalities and doing good."[56]

One example illustrating the radical or revolutionary intellectual alterations in American culture in the first half of the twentieth century pertains directly to philosophy, with implications for religion and theology. Although some observers seem to suggest that Dewey's instrumentalism represents a continuation and development of the American heritage as expressed by Jefferson, in reality, this twentieth-century philosopher-educator firmly rejected his predecessor' s views that certain moral and political truths were self-evident, and universally valid and desirable. By insisting upon a world of flux, denying all permanence, Dewey was committed to the position that the democratic way is preferable as far as it can be ascertained; the future must remain in doubt.[57] Jefferson struggled with the problem of reconciling "traditional" modes of thought (especially concerning morality) with modern scientism and empiricism (particularly in the form of the "French ideology" of his day),[58] while Dewey experienced no such kind of difficulty. Dewey, in his naturalistic empiricism, rejected substantial aspects of the earlier pragmatic tradition (as found in Peirce and James); the reconstruction he desired in philosophy (and in education) was radical, indeed, relative to previous developments in American philosophy (and education).[59]

A colleague of Dewey's, James H. Tufts, epitomizes this American intellectual revolution:

> "My generation has seen the passing of systems of thought which had reigned since Augustus. The conception of the world as a kingdom ruled by God, subject to his laws and their penalties, which had been undisturbed by the Protestant Reformation, has dissolved . . . The sanctions of our inherited morality have gone. Principles and standards which had stood for nearly two thousand years are gone."[60]

It is evident that, in this stage of the development of American thought, the narrowing of philosophical concerns from the metaphysical to antimetaphysical and exclusively empirical questions has been accompanied by a widespread process of secularization. The latter is clearly evident in Dewey's theory of the "religious," which culminates in his claim to have gone "beyond agnosticism." To him this means that he has established a philosophical posture which precludes even the possibility of raising a meaningful question of the existence of a Transcendent Being.[61] That he took American society in the same direction is clear from Commager's comment at mid-century that "it is scarcely an exaggeration to say that for a generation no major issue was clarified until Dewey had spoken."[62] However, while Dewey claimed to have gone "beyond agnosticism,"[63] others since have gone "beyond Dewey."

Without underestimating the continuing threads of nineteenth-century thought in the history of American philosophy since the cultural revolution near the turn of the century,[64] one can distinguish a new thrust since the original reactions against idealism. Clearly, the years from 1920 to 1970 are marked by ferment and variety.[65] The situation in the mid-1960s had been thoroughly pluralistic, characterized by the tendency "to draw upon a variety of philosophical traditions and to consider philosophy an ongoing cooperative enterprise in which all philosophers may participate and make some contribution."[66] Nevertheless, since 1960, a somewhat new direction in mainstream American philosophy seems to have developed in the aftermath of pragmatism, realism and naturalism. What is that new direction, and what does it mean for the present?

D. 1960–2000: THE SECOND PHASE

One of the differences between what appears to be stage one and stage two (after 1960) of American philosophy in the twentieth century pertains also to a similarity between them: the narrowing of the philosophical enterprise from its earlier attention (before 1900) to a relationship with theology; and to questions concerning the origin, meanings and ultimate destiny of life. Although the diminishment of the synoptic view was evident in the earlier years of the twentieth century, it assumed a different kind of posture somewhat later. One indication of a differentiation of two stages or levels lies in the observation that the specialization (coinciding with the professionalization) of twentieth-century American philosophy first was realized when philosophers began to focus exclusively upon epistemology and logic; later development was characterized by a specialization within epistemology and logic.[67]

The first phase is associated directly with pragmatism, realism, and naturalism, featuring a scientistic, empiricist orientation; the second phase is marked by a more widespread cultivation of logical positivism and linguistic analysis, the general tendency being the analytical. A related factor or corollary of the specialization in both phases was a lack of attention to public concerns; however, there appears to be a far more radical separation from social, political and related matters in the second phase than in the first for reasons which the following comments will attempt to clarify. This second stage or level of twentieth-century American philosophy developed out of the first. For example, the American philosophical movement called naturalism foreshadowed the later prominence of logical positivism in denying that there is a fundamental difference in aim and methodology between the natural sciences and "human studies" or social sciences. The naturalists were followed by logical positivists in the United States in insisting that in both areas the investigator must formulate hypotheses to be subjected to the test of empirical observation.[68]

In philosophical realism, epistemology was a focal point from the beginning; and in what became known as "new realism," the program for reforming philosophy closely resembled many features of analytic philosophy prevalent after mid-century. The new realists opposed speculative system building and mystical philosophy; dissociated philosophical research from the history of philosophy in favor of linking it with the "special sciences"; stressed extraordinary care in defining and using words; advocated logic and the method of analysis as the means of doing philosophy systematically; and urged dealing with philosophical problems one at a time, all this with the hope of creating some kind of consensus among philosophers.[69]

As observed above, earlier pragmatism (in Peirce and James) differed substantially from later modes (as in Dewey and his followers). Dewey's indifference even to the question of a transcendent being (in his attitude called "beyond agnosticism") seems to find a parallel in the secularizing by James. It has been observed that "the evolution of an areligious pragmatism did much to shape the problematic view of American intellectual history that historians and philosophers came to accept."[70] (This comment is not unrelated to the recent secularized treatments of Jefferson, Horace Mann and Maria Montessori in textbooks in education. Directly related to this statement is the recent tendency to diminish or dismiss the role of religion in the history of American higher education.)[71] Furthermore, pragmatism itself was not sustained among academic philosophers. It contributed to its own demise, of course, by eschewing general, speculative, synoptic questions in favor of immediate, specific, and resolvable problems, casting doubts upon the whole philosophic enterprise. In these circumstances, the social sciences tended to become the heirs of philosophy as means of resolving these problems of social organization, politics, education, and economic welfare.[72]

However, "The truth is that as we moved into the decade of the 'forties other influences were at work and they exerted pressure in new directions."[73] These influences included the writings of Bertrand Russell, G. E. Moore and subsequent analytic philosophers in the British neo-empiricist tradition. Combined with the invasion of continental positivism,[74] this signified skepticism about the role of reason in the conduct of human life; a decline in philosophical attention to broad human problems; a new emphasis upon logic, language, and the analysis of natural science to the exclusion of speculative matters; and concentration upon the accumulation of facts with the belief that somehow they would arrange and synthesize themselves, eliminating the need for rational explanations.[75] The two prime branches of recent analytic philosophy, logical positivism and linguistic analysis, deserve brief attention before turning to some direct practical consequences of these developments.

Logical positivism

> is a name assigned to the philosophical standpoint developed in the 1920's by a number of philosophers and scientists known as the Vienna Circle. This group was influenced by Bertrand Russell and Ludwig Wittgenstein; those among its leaders who either visited or moved permanently to the United States included Moritz Schlick, Herbert Feigl, Hans Reichenbach, Carl Hempel, and Alfred Tarski. As one observer notes, the presence of so many important representatives of this standpoint could not help but have significant repercussions on the American philosophical scene.[76]

One of the central postulates of logical positivism is called the Verifiability Principle, the principle that a proposition is cognitively meaningful *only* if it is empirically verifiable. The other key doctrine is that all sentences expressing necessary assertions, including logic and pure mathematics, are tautological. Following from these two theories is the conclusion that metaphysical pronouncements are literally nonsense because they are neither empirically verifiable nor purely formal. Traditional metaphysical judgments (as, for example, claims about the Absolute, transcendent values, material and spiritual substances, things-in-themselves, God, etc.) bear only "emotive" or "pictorial" meanings. Normative moral judgments are relegated to the "emotive theory." These positions of logical positivists effectively deny that traditional metaphysical and moral questions can be raised in any rationally meaningful manner.[77] Although it is extremely difficult to judge the extent to which these precise principles were held and taught in the United States, "the work of the logical positivists unquestionably produced a far more critical and suspicious attitude towards any kind of speculative philosophy . . . ."[78]

"Linguistic analysis" refers to "a number of somewhat heterogeneous philosophical tendencies"[79] associated with the efforts of British philosophers G. E. Moore, the later Wittgenstein, Gilbert Ryle and John Austin; and Americans Max Black and 0. K. Bouwsma. Although the linguistic analysts share little common doctrine and differ radically on questions such as those pertaining to determinism, dualism, and religion, they do seem to hold commonly "a special interest in ordinary language, a belief that by studying the ways in which words are used we can shed a great deal of light on philosophical problems and in many instances avoid becoming the victims of 'pseudo-problems.'"[80] The method frequently employed by these linguistic philosophers to analyze such words as "reason," "evidence," "cause," etc. is to examine a multitude of cases in which the word is used, along with the reasons for using it in the various circumstances. Although this "informal" approach probably is more widespread than others, a more "formal" approach (associated with the philosophies of Russell and Carnap, and preferred by Americans W. V. Quine and Nelson Goodman) also is employed.[81]

It is evident from these very brief surveys that one of the primary differences between the linguistic analysts and the logical positivists lies in their attitudes toward metaphysics. The former (in concurring with the latter) do not practice or advocate the practice of metaphysics; however, neither do they call it nonsense. They investigate the meanings of these "strange" assertions by employing their own methods for the purpose of clarification.[82] On the other hand, "Common to all forms of analytic philosophy has been the belief that philosophy has nothing of its own to add to our stock of knowledge; it is indeed a technique for talking about the logic and the grammar of the language used by others."[83]

This last statement is crucial to appreciating the current situation in American philosophy, and it distinguishes the second stage referred to above. In a certain sense, this analytic posture has resulted from and has substantiated facets of the earlier American neo-empiricism, but it has transcended previous twentieth-century American philosophies by proposing a position which can be described not only as "beyond agnosticism," but "beyond all world perspectives." It is diametrically opposed to all rational consideration of, or speculation about, life-oriented questions typical of the pre-twentieth-century American philosophies and their immediate successors in the earlier part of the twentieth century. This second stage, which has further delimited the scope of philosophy, also has carried its secularizing impact to a new level in that first order religious and theological questions are eliminated from rational investigation. The larger cultural background also has contributed to the reinforcement of an indifference toward these kinds of questions.

While some observers of this later phase of American philosophy in the twentieth century offer harsh criticism of this trend, Weiss does not despite his personal differences. Recognizing the "linguistic turn" of contemporary philosophy, he is not at all disturbed because "throughout history only a relatively few men have taken the categorical understanding of reality to be their primary concern."[84] He offers as an example the Middle Ages, during which Thomas Aquinas and Duns Scotus were among the few devoting themselves to philosophy in the broad sense, while hundreds of scholastics unknown today labored over highly specialized problems in logic and rhetoric.[85] However, on the other hand, it is obvious that the late twentieth-century United States has seen no Aquinas or Scotus! Furthermore, current American culture appears to be permeated by a social and popular indifference to philosophy, which would lead one to suggest that more forces than simply the history of American philosophy seem to be conspiring to the same end.

John E. Smith, referring critically to the American philosophical enterprise, notes two consequences of this "linguistic turn" or "the identification of philosophy with purely technical analysis":[86] 1) the loss of widespread interest in reading philosophical works, and 2) a loss of independence in philosophical reflection on the part of numerous American philosophers. The reasons for the dwindling of what was formerly a relatively broad audience lie in the irrelevance of typical philosophical problems to human living, the increasingly technical language of philosophical writings, and the lack of dialogue among representatives of differing philosophical positions. Unfortunately, according to Smith, since the broad philosophical issues do not "go away," and since education in philosophy is restricted to technical and methodological matters, those who do treat the "world views" do so without a proper education, and, therefore, without the discipline which brings comprehensive and internal coherence.[87]

The second consequence of the linguistic narrowing of American philosophical endeavors, a lack of independence, is attributed to a tendency of philosophers in the United States to imitate techniques and adopt principles of British philosophers without consideration for their own culture. Furthermore, the

> belief that philosophy begins and ends with the study of language has the effect of directing attention to what has *already been* expressed or articulated. The analysis of language, at least as carried on within the schools of linguistic philosophy, results in the disclosure of *past* thought and experience. . . . It leads to the neglect of *present* life and experience. . . . Failure to confront current experience means loss of independence in thinking; it means bondage to what others have already said.[88]

According to Smith, when "experience" is restricted to designating only a function supplying raw material for the natural sciences, reason itself is diminished. This leads to a bifurcation of fact and reason, and contributes to separating philosophy from life. He claims that "The more the philosophers of experience demanded a world of pure fact, of fact devoid of value or import, the more there opened up a chasm between fact and reason. As fact was more narrowly conceived, reason was more and more reduced to the status of empty form." "Experience, as brute fact, excludes reason; reason, as empty form, stands outside of experience. The two are connected in nothing but the most external fashion. The most serious immediate consequence is that reason is confined to its formal function and a general skepticism over the power of reason in practical life comes to prevail."[89]

Before proceeding to a summary and updating of this historical analysis of twentieth-century American philosophy, the pitfalls of our generalizations should be concretized. In brief, the point is that the development depicted herein, while apparently accurate enough for a wide sweep, is an approximation and overlooks specific individuals and philosophical movements which have no minor importance in the history of American thought. An example of an individual not sufficiently accounted for is Whitehead, and schools of philosophy (with their individual representatives) needing attention are Marxism, existentialism, phenomenology, later idealism, and Neo-Thomism.[90]

However, we do get a somewhat expanded version of the above account in Macquarrie's examination of the "frontier" (or boundary) of theology and philosophy[91] in twentieth-century thought in Western Civilization. According to this interpretation there are three phases or eras prior to the 1960s. The first phase or era of this frontier comprises ideas developed in the nineteenth century and continued (in influence) into the twentieth. The period is marked by a considerable variety of principles, in which, however, four common characteristics can be detected: 1) optimism or "a certain buoyancy of spirit"; 2) the idea of development (especially with a Hegelian or Darwinian flavor); 3) the dominance of the notion of "substance"—spiritual or material, but, in either case, signifying "solid enduring thinghood" as an explanatory model; and 4) comprehensiveness, referring to systematic treatment with an air of finality, and entailing a close association between theology and philosophy. The two general theological-philosophical orientations detected are (spiritualistic) idealism and naturalism.[92]

In the second phase of the development of the frontier between theology and philosophy in twentieth-century Western Civilization (according to Macquarrie), one discovers new movements belonging more properly to the twentieth century, which, however, have declined or have been transformed or differentiated into still more recent movements.[93] This transitional phase, exemplified by the new realism of Moore and Russell, is characterized by 1) pessimism; 2) the limitation of philosophy to some particular sector (as methodology), highlighted by the renunciation of metaphysics; and 3) an increasing divergence between theology and philosophy.[94]

No sharp dividing lines can be drawn between the first two phases of this history, and that is true also of the relationship between the second and third phases, the third being described as primarily a "continuation and accentuation of some of the tendencies" present in the second.[95] The second phase is said to have provided "the matrix out of which or against which arise those major forms of religious thought which have come to dominate the scene in the middle of our century."[96] Despite the presence of two major metaphysical schools of thought (realist metaphysics and neo-scholasticism, or, more particularly, neo-Thomism), the dominant temper of the mid-century years is said to have been anti-metaphysical.[97] Three noteworthy anti-metaphysical schools are logical empiricism (a later version of logical positivism, according to the terminology here), kerygmatic theology, and existentialism. The intensification of patterns established earlier leads Macquarrie to the conclusion that "the mid-century trends of religious thought reflect the outlook of a culture that has sailed into increasingly stormy weather as the century has proceeded, and that has become less and less sure of itself."[98]

A "Postscript" covering the decade of the 1960s is added in a revised edition of Macquarrie's book concerning the frontier of theology and philosophy in Western Civilization during the twentieth century. The only detail to be noted here concerns the question the author raises of the possibility of a new "watershed," characterized by the end of one phase without the benefit of the demarcation of a new era.[99] (It will be recalled that this historical analysis was initiated with the notion of a watershed, employed to portray the radical changes in the upheaval of American culture near the turn of the century.) This decade (1960–70), Macquarrie claims, is said to have witnessed rapid changes in religious thought, perhaps symptomatic of "unrest and probing of a very radical kind." Phrases such as "death of God," "secular Christianity," "black theology," "Dionysian religion," "new hermeneutic," "transcendental Thomism," and "theology of hope," so "roughly juxtaposed, tell something of the chaos and bewilderment in contemporary religious thought, reflecting, perhaps, chaos and bewilderment in the wider human society itself. But they also testify that religion and reflection upon religion are far from dead. They prove the point made at the end of the preceding chapter that 'the voyage goes on.'"[100] But did Macquarrie surmise that the voyage would go on to what has become known as postmodernism?

Although postmodernism is said to have been initiated by Friedrich Nietzsche (1844–1900), its impact on thought and life in the U.S. probably began in the 1960s. A very brief overview here will provide evidence of how its major effect reinforced the relativism so pervasive in late twentieth-century American intellectual life. While postmodernism defies definition, it does refer to a certain kind of "discontinuity with earlier phases of the modern period [prior to the 1960's], hence with the socio-cultural forms, or ideas and methods, characteristic of modern Western culture." It also has been called "the latest wave in the critique of the Enlightenment, the criticism of the principles characteristic of modern Western society that trace their legacy to the eighteenth century."[101]

Criticism of modernity in the twentieth century did not begin with postmodernism, of course. One example of a predecessor was the existentialism and phenomenology of French philosophers Sartre (1905–1980) and Merleau-Ponty (1908–1961). Their mode of critique, however, was different from the young French philosophers of the 1960s: Deleuze, Irigaray, Lyotard, Derrida and Foucault. This group had been educated by the leaders of another group known as structuralists, whose numbers included de Saussure, Jakobson and Levi-Strauss. The structuralists rejected the centrality of the self found in French existentialism and phenomenology; they sought structures above and beyond the individual person (as language, ritual, and kinship) which were thought to form the individual. Therefore, culture creates the self rather than vice versa; there is no original human nature against which a culture could be judged.[102] Structuralism appealed to many who found difficulty with the subjectivity of Sartre and Merleau-Ponty because it "seemed to offer the student of humanity a way of avoiding reduction to the natural sciences, while yet retaining objective, scientific methods . . . ."[103]

What was the response of the new French philosophers of the 1960s to this kind structuralism? They followed the rejection of the autonomous self, but the scientific pretensions they did not accept. They applied the analysis of human phenomena employed by the structuralists to the human sciences themselves because they saw them (the sciences) as human constructions. Thus, they became "post-structuralists" by radicalizing structuralism, thereby seeming to announce "the end of rational inquiry into truth, the illusory nature of any unified self, the impossibility of clear and unequivocal meaning, and the oppressive nature of all modern Western institutions."[104] They seemed to undermine all positive philosophical positions. This, plus radical disagreements among them, some of whom deny having specific principles or theories at all, leaves one wondering what "postmodernism" could possibly mean.

Nevertheless, as Cahoone observes, "understanding must begin somewhere."[105] He begins his characterization of postmodernism with the notion of complexity. That is, any conceptual scheme, rule, law, or basic distinction must fail—not only because of the limits of our knowledge, but "because of the nature of what is to be known."[106] There is no unitary origin or agency and, thus, no barriers among particular academic disciplines. Secondly, postmodernists deny "presence," or the claim of an "immediate relation of human judgments to what they judge."[107] While other philosophers have long denied the possibility of human cognitive access to reality, the postmodernists reject the purpose of epistemology, the whole enterprise of attempting to justify human knowledge. Thirdly, according to Cahoone, postmodernists are constructivists in regard to knowledge: human beings create their own representations, which always require a selection from a phenomenal complexity, which involves a suppression of some aspect(s)—which (suppression) itself is covered up. Therefore, so-called truth is a necessary product of misrecognition or error.[108]

The fourth feature of postmodernism described by Cahoone is the "immanence of norms": "the norms we use to judge are themselves products of the processes they judge."[109] In other words, there are no norms in ethics or any other area of life which are outside or independent of nature, signs, experience, or social interests. Fifthly and finally, postmodernists employ an "analytic strategy which is the complex application of the four themes [above] . . . ."[110] This is not unrelated to the repression and exclusion featured in the third characteristic above, and constitutes a political approach insofar as major attention is afforded the "margins of the text," the elements (of a social system, for example) that tend to be habitually overlooked by mainstream observers. This "deconstruction" of the text tends to reveal its fallaciousness, instability, and (in some instances) its immorality.[111]

These five general features of post-modernist thought, when combined with what has been called a "notoriously difficult writing style,"[112] convey the image of a world-view which might be described as "beyond relativism." While most postmodernists likely would reject Cahoone's characterization, they apparently also would reject relativism because of its pretension to knowledge of relative truths. In any case, this pattern of reflection contributes to the rejection of truth as founded in God, nature, or reason. It also assists in appreciating various popular notions of life and living such as the following: "'It is time now to get serious about religion—all religion—and draw a firm line between the real world and the world of dreams.'" Along with religion, all truth is debunked: "'There's a sort of comfort in knowing that . . . I don't have to have the answers, and that there aren't necessarily answers.'"[113] As for the future of postmodernism, Connor asserts that it "has indeed shown an extraordinary capacity to renew itself in the conflagration of its demise."[114]

E. CONCLUDING REMARKS

The selected aspects of this overview of the history of American philosophy since the late nineteenth century fit with extraordinary congruence into the history of the frontiers of theology and philosophy in Western Civilization during a similar period as depicted by Macquarrie. There are some differences, of course, due to the variations in the scope of content and geography. For various reasons, the philosophical scene in the United States seems to reflect the problems of the larger landscape in intensified fashion. Identification of some of those specific problems will establish the climate for the second section of the paper, concerning the teaching of philosophy in Catholic higher education.

In the elaboration of the philosophical revolution of the late nineteenth and early twentieth centuries and its aftermath, it becomes evident that sufficient (but cautious) generalization reveals two phases or levels of philosophical development since the turn of the century. The reactions against nineteenth century idealism in the forms of pragmatism, realism, and naturalism (occurring within the first three decades of this century) emphasize logic and epistemology, and are seen to exude a scientific and empiricist spirit; they represent a narrowing and secularizing trend relative to the earlier life-oriented, religious philosophies. While these modes of thought, including idealism, did not fade away entirely, a new emphasis began to appear long before, but especially after, World War II. In this second phase or level, certainly continuous with the first in some ways, a new analytic temper of mind sparked a widespread opposition to rational consideration of, or speculation about, synoptic world-views, and normative and prescriptive principles which were so prominent even into early twentieth-century American philosophy. After World War II attention was directed primarily to carefully defined and isolated questions of meaning in scientific and ordinary language *within* logic and epistemology by philosophers who had become known as logical positivists and linguistic analysts.

While there is no particular year in American thought in which the influence of this more recent orientation can be said to have "ascended" (despite the publication of *Mind and World-Order* by C.I. Lewis in 1929), its prominence does represent a new *level* of the narrowing and secularizing trend of the earlier twentieth century. In regard to the narrowing, it is evident that the shift to the exclusively empirical, which provided a basis for Dewey's position called "beyond agnosticism," was overshadowed by the movement in which philosophy was carried to a position "beyond world perspectives," as just described. The accompanying secularization not only eliminated from rational investigation authentically religious and theological questions (which Dewey's position had achieved), but it also eliminated all possibility of inquiring philosophically even into *natural* responses to life-oriented matters (which Dewey had proposed), thereby creating a wider scope of indifference to religion and theology, as well as a more intense form of opposition.[115]

It can be presumed that the confusion observed in 1980[116] has not dissipated entirely. Aiken, in recognizing the very limited role of analytic philosophy, sees even that as due to be rejected: "The great thing is to rid ourselves once for all of philosophical dictators and ideologues who presume to tell their fellows by what 'principles' their institutions are to be governed. In short, as some begin to argue, we are now entering the age of counter-ideology in which the whole enterprise of philosophy is finally to be consigned to the outer darkness."[117] Was he forecasting the postmodernist movement? In a lengthier passage, Aiken points to the same conclusion, but in a manner emphasizing the confusion, not only in philosophy, but, at least potentially, in society at large:

> What remains for the conscientious philosopher in the modern world to do? What can be his vocation? Let us make no mistake: if there are principles of science, no philosopher can any longer pretend that there are distinctive principles of philosophy. Even to speak, at this late date, of the principles of metaphysics, or of epistemology, or of ethics is tantamount to inciting one's fellow philosophers to riot. The traditional academic quadrivium of metaphysics, epistemology, logic, and ethics has been shaken to its foundations. General metaphysics and epistemology have become, at best, ideology, and ideology itself, as we have seen, is now in increasing disrepute. Who shall presume to tell us, as the old metaphysicians hoped to do, what are the eternal and pervasive elements or categories of being? Who shall instruct us, as the old epistemologist hoped to do, in the universal principles of human knowledge? Logic, by general consent, is no longer a philosophical subject, and all self-respecting logicians are, or wish they were, members of the department of mathematics. As for ethics or "moral philosophy"—it has gone the way of all analytical philosophical studies and

wound up as "meta-ethics," a study which presumably will find its own proper niche in the new science of linguistics.[118]

The development of postmodernist thought alongside later forms of logical empiricism and linguistic analysis obviously has done nothing to rejuvenate philosophy—unless going "beyond relativism" can be considered a rejuvenation! The quest for (even radically relative) truth has been abandoned by the postmodernists because they see no basis for it. The traditional Western emphases upon or allusions to God, Nature, and Reason as sources and foundations of truth are abandoned.

What remains? That question symbolizes the bewilderment in "an age of anxiety" in Western Civilization: "The future of Western culture is put in question—as perhaps it ought to be. Indeed, the future of mankind is in question—..."[119] Perhaps the most crucial factor is a tendency toward the loss of self-identity: "This is the age when man has become fully and thoroughly problematic to himself."[120] This state of affairs is not unconnected, of course, to such noteworthy factors characterizing the development of twentieth-century philosophy in the United States as the following: extremely technical language, a lack of relevance to daily human living, a deficiency of social and political leadership, increasing indifference to history, reductionistic orientations, pessimism (that is, a certain malaise of the spirit), and failure to capitalize upon the values of Christianity. Several of these features have contributed directly to the diminishment of an audience for philosophy, now limited almost exclusively to professionals.

We noticed above that the professionalization of American philosophy in the twentieth century contributed immensely to the tendency within the field toward narrowing the scope of issues and toward secularization. However, it appears that a far more fundamental factor, internal to the process of philosophizing itself, is the disillusionment (increasing dramatically with the onset of "modern" philosophy) deriving directly from the lack of consensus and the consequent lack of certitude, resulting from attempting to answer metaphysical and related questions. Apparently foundational to the development of this tendency toward a radical lack of agreement was (and is) the separation of traditional religions (especially Christianity in Western Civilization) from the philosophical enterprise. In terms of a Christian interpretation of reality, the twentieth-century development of American philosophy toward bankruptcy is not very surprising at all. In fact, it could have been expected simply by noticing the increasing separation of faith from reason and theology from philosophy.

To suggest now that the only "hope" for philosophy is to renew its relationship to religion and theology is to invite vociferous objections, of course. Some of these objections cannot be addressed directly from a Christian perspective because they embody the impossibility of such a perspective. Other objections testify to the complexity of the matter even for the Christian. Nevertheless, it is contended here that doing philosophy in a mode compatible with, and in relationship to, principles of Christianity and the Catholic Church is a legitimate option, and that a vital dimension of that mode is serious attention to the history of philosophy.

While the redirection of contemporary American philosophy cannot be expected to occur quickly or through the efforts of a single social agency, it does not appear presumptuous to assert that American Catholic universities hold a key to unlocking the grip of widespread indifference to philosophy (and theology). The next section of this treatise is intended to explain this assertion through a summary and analysis of principles of Pope John Paul II concerning the ideal of a Catholic university. These principles (I contend) can be applied to circumstances in the United States in a manner enabling Americans to confront the critical challenges of the twenty-first century, thereby capitalizing upon a dramatic opportunity matched by a desperate cultural need.

NOTES

1. Paul Kurtz, "Introduction," *American Thought Before 1900: A Sourcebook from Puritanism to Darwinism*, ed. Paul Kurtz (New York: The Macmillan Company; London: Collier-Macmillan, Ltd., 1966), 15–16.

2. Ibid., 16.

3. Ibid.

4. Ibid., 17. For a lengthy study of this matter, see David F. Bowers (ed.), *Foreign Influences in American Life: Essays and Critical Bibliographies* (New York: Peter Smith, 1952).

5. The St. Louis Hegelians, under the leadership of Henry C. Brockmeyer (1828–1906) and William Torrey Harris (1835–1909), became the most renowned group of idealists, with the assistance of the *Journal of Speculative Philosophy* (the first philosophical journal in the United States), founded and edited by Harris from 1867–1880. Undoubtedly, the best known individual American idealist has been Josiah Royce (1855–1916). Transcendentalism was closely allied to philosophical idealism, but tended toward a literary and romantic, rather than a technical, approach to philosophy.

See Kurtz, "Introduction," *American Thought Before 1900 . . . ,*" ed. Kurtz, 28–30. Some pertinent sources include the following: *The American Hegelians: An Intellectual Episode in the History of Western America*, edited by William H. Goetzmann, with the assistance of Dickson Pratt (New York: Alfred A. Knopf, 1973); Henry A. Pochmann, *New England Transcendentalism and St. Louis Hegelianism* (Philadelphia: Carl Schurz Memorial Foundation, 1948); Charles M. Perry, *The St.*

Louis Movement in Philosophy (Norman, Oklahoma: University of Oklahoma Press, 1930); Francis B. Harmon, *The Social Philosophy of the St. Louis Hegelians* (New York: Columbia University Press, 1943); Loyd D. Easton, *Hegel's First American Followers, the Ohio Hegelians: J.B. Stallo, Peter Kaufmann, Moncure Conway, August Willich* (Athens, OH: Ohio University Press, 1966); Denton J. Snider, *The St. Louis Movement in Philosophy* (St. Louis: Sigma Publishing Company, 1920); and Henry A. Pochmann, *German Culture in America* (Madison, WI: University of Wisconsin Press, 1957).

6. Henry Steele Commager, *The American Mind: An Interpretation of American Thought and Character Since the 1880's* (New Haven: Yale University Press, 1950), 41.

7. Ibid., 53.

8. Ibid., 44.

9. Ibid., 41.

10. Henry Steele Commager, "Portrait of the American," *Years of the Modern: An American Appraisal,* edited by J.W. Chase (New York: Longmans, Green and Company, 1949), 6–8.

11. Commager, *The American Mind . . .* , 407.

12. Ibid., 43. See also 50.

13. David F. Bowers, "Hegel, Darwin, and the American Tradition," *Foreign Influences in American Life: Essays and Critical Bibliographies,* edited by David F. Bowers (New York: Peter Smith, 1952), 148.

14. Ibid., 148–52.

15. Commager, *The American Mind . . .* , 162.

16. Ibid., 162–63.

17. For example, see Ibid., 86–88.

18. According to Bowers, "Although Darwinism achieved the greater notoriety because of its more obviously dramatic implications, Hegelianism also had a popular following—particularly among the German-Americans of the Middle West—and, so far as its ultimate effects were concerned, was to be no less important." Bowers, "Hegel, Darwin, and the American Tradition," *Foreign Influences in American Life*, edited by Bowers, 153.

19. Ibid., 147.

20. Ibid., 147, 152–59, 162–63.

21. Bowers' conclusion of the matter is as follows: "There was, in short, a broad but genuine sense in which the influence of Hegel and that of Darwin were able to reinforce each other and to offer a common opposition to the previous pattern of American thought. And this is what actually occurred in the thinking of a number of influential critics who happened to be subjected to both influences." Ibid., 163.

22. Ibid., 159–64. An important and interesting point here concerns Hegel's presumed support of Christian revelation, when, in fact, he was not an orthodox Christian and apparently contributed significantly to a demise of the influence of Christianity in Western Civilization. See Ibid., 161. (In fact, Hegel has been referred to as the "grandfather of modern atheism.")

23. Ibid., 159–68.

24. In fact, Dewey published an essay entitled "The Influence of Darwin on Philosophy." See John Dewey, *The Influence of Darwin on Philosophy: and Other Essays in Contemporary Thought* (New York: Peter Smith, 1951), 1–19. (Originally published in 1910 by Henry Holt and Company.)

25. One of the effects of the American intellectual revolution under discussion was the tendency toward a separation of theology and philosophy, anticipated much earlier, of course, through Descartes and other modern Continental and British thinkers.

26. W.H. Werkmeister, *A History of Philosophical Ideas in America* (New York: The Ronald Press Company, 1949), vi.

27. Kurtz, "Introduction," *American Thought Before 1900* . . . , ed. Kurtz, 28–30. See also *The American Hegelians* . . . , edited by Goetzmann. A somewhat extended elaboration of the absolutist-personalist poles of idealistic thought can be found in John Macquarrie, *Twentieth Century Religious Thought: The Frontiers of Philosophy and Theology, 1900–1970*, revised edition (London: SCM Press, Ltd., 1971), 23–57.

28. Kurtz, "Introduction," *American Thought Before 1900* . . . , ed. Kurtz, 30. Kurtz seems to be referring to absolute idealism in this statement; however, for an account this generalized, the distinction is of little importance.

29. Paul Kurtz, "Introduction," *American Philosophy in the Twentieth Century: A Sourcebook from Pragmatism to Philosophical Analysis*, ed. Paul Kurtz (New York: The Macmillan Company; London: Collier-Macmillan, Ltd., 1966), 18.

30. Kurtz, "Introduction," *American Thought Before 1900* . . . , ed. Kurtz, 30.

31. For a brief commentary on the religious and idealistic features of early pragmatism, see Bruce Kuklick, *The Rise of American Philosophy: Cambridge, Massachusetts, 1860–1930* (New Haven and London: Yale University Press, 1977), xix-xxi, xxiii, 26–27, 56–67.

32. Ibid., 58, 400–01.

33. One means of discussing the similar, but differing, principles of representatives of a school of philosophy is found in depicting the *spirit* of a particular philosophical movement. This approach is exemplified in Frederick Copleston, S.J., *Contemporary Philosophy: Studies of Logical Positivism and Existentialism* (Paramus, NJ, and New York: Newman Press, 1966; first published in 1956), especially pp. 125–47 (concerning existentialism); and in John E. Smith, *The Spirit of American Philosophy*, Revised edition (Albany: State University of New York Press, 1983).

34. Kurtz, "Introduction," *American Philosophy in the Twentieth Century* . . . , ed. Kurtz, 78.

35. Ibid.

36. Ibid., 21–22.

37. Ibid., 22–24.

38. Ibid., 26–27.

39. Ibid., 187–88.

40. Ibid., 188.

41. Kuklick, 27.

42. Ibid., 59.

43. Ibid., xvii. It is pointed out that the "watershed document" is *Mind and World-Order* by C.I. Lewis, published in 1929, and that the major Harvard philosophers of that time were read primarily within the philosophic community. See also p. xvi.

44. Ibid., 27.

45. Ibid., xxv, 452.

46. Ibid., xvi.

47. Ibid., xxv, xviii.

48. Ibid., xxv.

49. Ibid., xxiii. Dewey is an obvious exception to at least one aspect of this point. (See Commager, *The American Mind* . . . , 99.) However, Kuklick's book pertains only to Cambridge philosophy and philosophers, and, therefore, excludes Dewey from consideration. On the other hand, it is claimed that "the history of philosophy in Cambridge from the Civil War to the Great Depression illuminates the history of American thought as a whole: *it* is a history of Harvard writ large. Moreover, the story of the professionalization of philosophy at Harvard epitomizes the professionalization of the academy in twentieth-century America." Kuklick, xxvii.

50. The claim here is not that scientism and empiricism necessarily precipitated pessimism and meaninglessness (although, from certain religious points of view, that argument could be expected), but that these phenomena were, in fact, juxtaposed in American culture.

51. Commager, *The American Mind* . . . , 103.

52. Ibid., 106.

53. Werkmeister, vi.

54. Commager, *The American Mind* . . . , 163.

55. These observations are based upon Commager's assertions in *The American Mind* . . . , 163, 165–67.

56. Ibid., 168.

57. Bowers, "Hegel, Darwin, and the American Tradition," *Foreign Influences in American Life* . . . , ed. Bowers, 168–69.

58. See Adrienne Koch, *The Philosophy of Thomas Jefferson* (Chicago: Quadrangle Books, University of Chicago Press, 1964).

59. According to Bowers, " . . . Dewey's philosophy, far from representing a logical development of what was implicit in the American tradition to begin with, is actually an innovation, a radical reinterpretation of that tradition in monistic, relativistic, and institutional terms." Bowers, "Hegel, Darwin, and the American Tradition," *Foreign Influences in American Life,* ed. Bowers, 169.

60. Cited by Commager, *The American Mind* . . . , 106.

61. John Dewey, *A Common Faith* (New Haven: Yale University Press, 1934).

62. Commager, *The American Mind* . . . , 100.

63. For a related point of view, see an interpretation of Auguste Comte's thought in a chapter entitled "Beyond Atheism": Henri DeLubac, S.J., *The Drama of Atheist Humanism,* tr. Edith M. Riley (Cleveland and New York: Meridian Books, The World Publishing Company, 1963; original copyright: Sheed and Ward, Inc., 1950), 91–97.

64. For some remarks concerning the continuity throughout modern and contemporary philosophy in Western Civilization, see Henry D. Aiken, "The Fate

of Philosophy in the Twentieth Century," *Philosophy in the Twentieth Century: An Anthology*, eds. William Barrett and Henry D. Aiken, Vol. 1 (New York: Random House, 1962), 4–10.

65. Peter Bertocci, "Preface," *Mid-Twentieth Century American Philosophy: Personal Statements*, ed. Peter Bertocci (New York: Humanities Press, 1974), vii.

66. Kurtz, "Introduction," *American Philosophy in the Twentieth Century* . . . , 41.

67. Kuklick, 452.

68. Kurtz, "Introduction," *American Philosophy in the Twentieth Century* . . . , 34–35.

69. Ibid., 23–24. See also Kuklick, 566.

70. See Kuklick, 567.

71. Concerning the treatment of religion in the history of higher education in the United States, see *The Secularization of the Academy*, eds. George M. Marsden and Bradley J. Longfield (New York and Oxford: Oxford University Press, 1992); George M. Marsden, *The Soul of the American University: From Protestant Establishment to Established Nonbelief* (New York: Oxford University Press, 1994); and George M. Marsden, *The Outrageous Idea of Christian Scholarship* (Oxford, New York: Oxford University Press, 1997).

72. Smith, 199.

73. Ibid., 198.

74. Reference to such currents from abroad also is found in Kuklick, 566. The Vienna Circle and Wittgenstein also are specifically mentioned here.

75. Kuklick, 198–99.

76. Kurtz, "Introduction," *American Philosophy in the Twentieth Century* . . . , 33. (See also p. 32.) Furthermore, there were also Americans as C.I. Lewis and P.W. Bridgman who developed strikingly similar principles independently of the University of Vienna philosophers. (See p. 34.)

77. Ibid., 33–34.

78. Ibid., 34. Of course, this mode of philosophy also raised questions which had been seriously neglected previously.

79. Ibid., 36.

80. Ibid.

81. Ibid., 36–37.

82. Ibid., 36.

83. Smith, 200.

84. Paul Weiss, "The Philosophic Quest," *Mid-Twentieth Century American Philosophy* . . . , ed. Bertocci, 240.

85. Ibid.

86. Smith, 200.

87. Ibid., 200–03.

88. Ibid., 204.

89. Ibid., 209. Despite the gloomy overall picture, Smith finds some hope for a change of philosophical venue on three bases: 1) a renewed interest in speculative philosophy rooted in an awareness of the inevitability of raising fundamental questions such as the nature and meaning of freedom and responsibility, the idea of

history, and the concept of God; 2) a growing concern among college-age students for the broader speculative questions and problems of ethics and religion; and 3) a revival of interest in problems, such as those of religion, with clear philosophical bearings. This whole section reflecting Smith's views is based upon his remarks in *The Spirit of American Philosophy* (Ibid.), 197–210.

90. For references to Whitehead and these modes of philosophy in relationship to American culture, see Kurtz, "Introduction," *American Philosophy in the Twentieth Century* . . . , 30–32, 37–41.

91. The "territory" of Macquarrie's historical analysis is "religious thought," signifying "all serious reflection of a philosophical nature on the central themes of religion." It includes *philosophy of religion* ("that branch of philosophy which concerns itself with interpreting and evaluating religion") and *philosophical theology* ("that branch of theology which concerns itself with elucidating and examining the philosophical implications of a religious faith"). Macquarrie, 15.

92. This idealism is of two basic modes: critical (or neo-Kantian) idealism and speculative (or neo-Hegelian) idealism. The latter type is comprised of absolute idealism and personal idealism. A general account of the first phase or era is found in Ibid., 18–22, 116.

93. These movements have roots in the nineteenth century, but exerted their greatest influence after 1900. They have not necessarily lost vitality, but their original formulations have been superseded or have faded into the background. Ibid., 118–19.

94. A general summary of the second phase or era is located in Ibid., 18, 117–20.

95. Ibid., 120. On p. 18, Macquarrie remarks that these tendencies of the third phase "hold the field at the present time." However, that statement is a part of the first edition of 1961, which was revised and expanded in a 1971 edition.

96. Ibid., 252–53.

97. "Metaphysics" here refers to the strict meaning, "an intellectual discipline, a rational speculation about ultimate reality." Ibid., 253–54.

98. Ibid., 253. The overview of this phase is found in Ibid., 18, 120, 252–56.

99. These remarks (Ibid., 377) can be related to the hope for the future seen by Smith in regard to the American intellectual milieu (observed in a footnote above).

100. Macquarrie, 377.

101. Lawrence Cahoone, "Introduction," *From Modernism to Postmodernism: An Anthology*, Ed. Lawrence Cahoone, Expanded Second Edition (Oxford: Blackwell Publishing, 2003), 2.

102. Ibid., 3–4.

103. Ibid., 4.

104. Ibid.

105. Ibid., 10.

106. Ibid.

107. Ibid.

108. Ibid., 10–11.

109. Ibid., 11.

110. Ibid.

111. Ibid., 11–12.

112. Ibid., 12.

113. Citations by Thomas B. Woods, Jr., "None So Blind: How Secularists Ignore the Value of Religion," *Crisis: Politics, Culture, and the Church*, 23 (November, 2005), 28.

114. Steven Conner, "Introduction," *The Cambridge Companion to Postmodernism*, Ed. Steven Connor (Cambridge: University Press, 2004), 1.

115. Dewey contributed directly to the positivistic and linguistic outlook concerning the question of the existence of God in his attitude designated by the epithet "beyond agnosticism." He also indirectly encouraged the replacement of philosophy by the social sciences by the manner in which he carried on his philosophical activity. Nevertheless, he did not consciously and directly relegate philosophy to purely technical and methodological procedures for analyzing *de facto* propositions; his intention was diametrically opposed to this as is illustrated in his philosophy of education. He wished to unite philosophy and life, and, in this regard, only inadvertently, it seems, did he contribute to the essential feature of the second (analytic) phase of twentieth-century American philosophy.

116. A glance at mail received in 1980 confirms the tendencies elaborated above. For example, notice of a book (*Education and Values*, edited by Douglas Sloan and published by Teachers College Press) with a 1980 publication date reads, in part: "Education and educators must become aware of the present breach between knowledge and values and realize that a transformation is in order that will once again include ethical and religious beliefs and emotive perceptions in the domain of reason."

Another example is a communication received from the Center for Process Studies in Claremont, California, postmarked February 18, 1980. In the letter encouraging membership in the Center, which promotes especially the investigation of the thought of Whitehead, there is a call for cultivating "post-modern" thought (such as that of Whitehead) against "the deleterious consequences of modern thought that are becoming increasingly obvious." Those consequences include the following: 1) in ontology, the untenable choice (for the scientifically alert) between reductionistic materialism or unintelligible dualism; 2) in epistemology, the position that assertions about "so-called" ethical, aesthetic, and religious dimensions of experience are devoid of truth value and closed to rational arbitration; and 3) concerning philosophy of religion and theology, the insistence that there is no possibility of divine activity in the world, or, at least, no possibility of discussing it intelligibly. Another charge against modern (presumably meaning "contemporary") philosophy in this circular is that it has remained at a high level of abstraction, failing to contend with the concrete problems of the time. (The letter supplying these observations is signed by the Director, the Executive Director, and the Director of Development of the Center for Process Studies, 1325 North College Avenue, Claremont, California 91711.)

117. Aiken, "The Fate of Philosophy in the Twentieth Century," *Philosophy in the Twentieth Century . . .* , eds. Barrett and Aiken, Vol. 1, 15.

118. Ibid., 16–17.

119. Macquarrie, 253.

120. Max Scheler, cited by Barrett, "The Twentieth Century in Its Philosophy," *Philosophy in the Twentieth Century . . .* , edited by Barrett and Aiken, Vol. 1, 25.

Chapter Two

Teaching Philosophy in a Catholic University according to John Paul II

The Apostolic Constitution *Ex Corde Ecclesiae* was promulgated in 1990 by Pope John Paul II. To appreciate this document in greater depth, one can consult his Encyclical Letters *Veritatis splendor* (1993) and *Fides et ratio* (1998); they elaborate primarily the ethical and the intellectual dimensions, respectively, of the Catholic university, which is the focus of the letter of 1990.[1] Since the author of these three documents holds that the center of Catholicism, Jesus Christ, Who is God, also is the center of the Catholic university, it appears that theology becomes the focal point of the educational process in this kind of institution. However, philosophy also occupies a central place because of its natural relationship to theology (and to all the other arts and sciences), and because of its role in the heritage of the Roman Catholic Church. We will consider his comments pertaining to philosophy in accord with seven themes representing basic principles found primarily in Part I, "Identity and Mission," but also in the "Introduction" of *Ex Corde Ecclesiae*. In Part II, "General Norms," John Paul II addresses practical applications of principles from the "Introduction" and Part I. These seven themes include the following: 1) the search for truth and meaning, 2) the integration of knowledge in teaching and research, 3) the dialogue between faith and reason, 4) academic freedom, 5) the moral dimension of academic life—in relationship to the intellectual side, 6) the academic community, and 7) human nature.

A. THE SEARCH FOR TRUTH AND MEANING

In the "Introduction" to *Ex Corde Ecclesiae*, John Paul II specifies the focal point of the academic enterprise called a Catholic university, namely, truth.

The centrality of the notion of truth in this forty-eight page document cannot be overestimated. The term itself occurs fourteen times in the first six pages, and its meaning and spirit pervade every sentence of the whole document. These facts alone alert us to the necessity and importance of philosophy in the Catholic university (which, of course, incorporates the undergraduate college and, in the American context, includes the Catholic college which is not integral to a Catholic university). The term "meaning" also is used in conjunction with truth. For example, the author refers to "the urgent need of . . . *proclaiming the meaning of truth*, that fundamental value without which freedom, justice and human dignity are extinguished" (ECE, Intro., 4).

This first theme, "the search for truth and meaning," highlights also the process of searching, which John Paul II in *Ex Corde Ecclesiae* emphasizes. The term "search" occurs eight times in the first eight pages of the document; it conveys not only a process relative to truth and meaning, but also the finitude and incompleteness of human nature. Human beings actualize themselves as persons only by possessing truth and meaning—which requires a continuous search. But, isn't God in His everlasting glory complete and absolute, and isn't this reality demanded to fulfill human persons? The answer to both queries is positive. However, the author of *Ex Corde Ecclesiae* clarifies a distinction frequently overlooked. He says that the Catholic university must attempt "to unite existentially through intellectual acumen two orders of reality which appear antithetical: the search for truth and the certainty of already knowing the fount of truth" (ECE, Intro., 1), later referred to obliquely as "courageous creativity" and "rigorous fidelity" (ECE, Intro., 8). The continuous search is necessary, of course, because of our persistently limited knowledge; the fount of truth is the infinite God Himself in His everlasting glory, Who is Truth. The same distinction can be explained in terms of immanence and transcendence. God, Who in Himself is transcendent (beyond time and change) can become immanent, that is, known by human persons in the world; the former is permanent, the latter changing. Therefore, there are eternal *truths*, but no eternal *expressions* of truth. This distinction applies to Judaism and Islam as well as to Christianity, of course. It also applies to the philosophies of Socrates, Plato and Aristotle. In any case, it is a philosophical matter to be utilized in the overall enlightenment of all students in a Catholic university. *How* is this distinction (and the search for truth and meaning, in general) to be inculcated in students? The next two topics address this question directly and reflect two essential features of research (and teaching) in the Catholic university according to John Paul II: seeking an "integration of knowledge," and pursuing a "dialogue between faith and reason" (ECE, I, 15).

B. THE INTEGRATION OF KNOWLEDGE IN TEACHING AND RESEARCH

Plato provides a clue to the difficulties of learning and the effort required in his analogy of the cave in Book VII of the *Republic*: the ascent out of the cave (darkness) to the sun (light) is uphill and steep. Rigorous thinking is no day at the beach! One of the reasons for this is our discursive powers of understanding: since we become aware of truth only by parts or aspects, the integration of knowledge in the teaching-learning process becomes a crucial matter in the Catholic university. What does this mean, and what are the means to it? First of all, particular academic disciplines in the "circle of the arts and sciences" must be studied independently of each other and then interrelated. Theology has a special place in this process because its focus is upon God, the source of all things. However, philosophy is necessary, too, because of its larger perspective; philosophy studies all things and their interrelationships from the point of view of their ultimate meaning. Therefore, especially through the study of theology and philosophy, faculty and students (in their respective roles) must exert "a constant effort to determine the relative place and meaning of each of the various disciplines within the context of the human person and the world that is enlightened by the Gospel, and therefore by a faith in Christ . . . as the centre of creation and of human history" (ECE, I, 16).

A crucial theological and philosophical principle underlying the pedagogical necessities in pursuing an integration of knowledge is the unity of truth. John Paul II claims that the oneness of truth is "a basic postulate of human reason, which finds expression in the principle of non-contradiction" (FR, 34). Further evidence lies in the fact that God is One and is the Creator of the world. Since God and the world (including human creatures) are the objects of knowledge, all truths must be interconnected and incapable of internal contradiction. As a result, therefore, of the limitations of human discursive learning, the curriculum (literally, the path to the truth) must be comprised of discrete academic disciplines (each with its proper first principles, methods, and conclusions). These disciplines must be interrelated in order to facilitate discovery of the whole truth, insofar as possible. In summary, the integration of knowledge by pursuing each academic discipline in relationship to all others and all disciplines in relationship to the final end of life, represents an essential responsibility of the Catholic university in assisting students to employ their cognitive abilities (with attending *subjective* features) in attaining awareness of *objective* truth.

C. THE DIALOGUE BETWEEN FAITH AND REASON

Pope John Paul II insists that this integration of knowledge in the Catholic university through the cooperative efforts of teachers (as helpers) and students cannot be achieved without "a dialogue between faith and reason, so that it can be seen more profoundly how faith and reason bear harmonious witness to the unity of all truth" (ECE, I, 17). This initiates the third topic, pertaining to how reason properly employed in philosophy leads one to religious faith, which then is to be further appreciated by the utilization of philosophy. For the sake of clarification, we will take "reason" to be intelligent articulation by means of distinguishing wholes from their parts; by proceeding from one proposition to another (as premises to conclusions or causes to effects); or by the original cognizance of a situation. There are various kinds of reasoning (displayed in the academic disciplines), from which philosophy is distinct by its attempts to know and to formulate the comprehensive whole, and by its concern with first principles, namely the divine.[2] On the other hand, knowing by faith signifies accepting conceptions or conclusions on the authority of another on the basis of one's trust in the witness of the other. As used here, faith usually refers to trust in God (supernatural faith), but it can refer to faith in a human being (natural faith). The academic discipline of theology employs both faith and reason. Theological reflection begins with conceptions and propositions based on faith, which are then investigated by reason, particularly philosophical reason.

In the Encyclical Letter *Fides et ratio*, Pope John Paul II adverts to several means of separating reason from faith, all of which result in the diminution of meaning in human living because they lead to skepticism and eventually to nihilism. The resulting emphasis on feeling and experience signifies a distrust in reason. Examples of philosophy separated from faith are positivistic and directly atheistic approaches to philosophy. Therefore, while it would be important to teach these modes of philosophy in a Catholic university, it would be improper to include *only* these in the philosophy curriculum. On the other hand, according to the author of *Fides et ratio*, philosophy can and does lead one to faith. The reason for this is that "in the deepest recesses of the human heart there has been sown [by God] a burning desire for God." Therefore, the Catholic university should cultivate "reason's capacity to rise beyond passing things and journey abroad into the infinite" (FR, 24). This can be achieved in many academic fields, of course, but especially in philosophy.

In this same document, John Paul II stresses the principle that faith needs reason. Therefore, theology requires the assistance of philosophy, a philosophy autonomous and open to transcendence, of course. As reason can aid faith, so philosophy can aid theology, for example, in understanding Biblical or other revealed truths. While reason can reach some truths without the aid of faith—meaning that philosophy in itself is a valuable and necessary discipline in the curriculum of the Catholic university—religious faith also can aid reason. That is, philosophy is abetted by its association with theology (while remaining clearly distinct from theology) by being opened to a wider perspective, to a higher realm, toward its ultimate end. Because of the importance of love in knowing (we wish to know what we love), faith in God, which necessarily involves love, spurs reason to continue or even to intensify its activity in knowing (FR, 41, 42, 73).

Finally, concerning this topic of the dialogue between faith and reason, John Paul II emphasizes their mutuality and fundamental harmony. He promotes a "mutual interchange" between philosophy and theology in what amounts to a summary of the central theme of *Fides et ratio*: "The fundamental harmony between philosophical knowledge and the knowledge of faith is once again confirmed: faith demands that its objects be understood with the help of reason; reason, in attaining the summit of its search, unavoidably points to what faith makes plain" (FR, 42). Implications of these principles for teaching philosophy in the Catholic university are unmistakable. Philosophy must be taught, and it must be studied by *all* students. The content and the teaching of the curriculum in philosophy must be conducive to opening the minds of students to transcendence. Philosophy must be distinguished from theology, but also must be taught in relationship to theology—as well as to all other academic disciplines. The philosophy faculty in the Catholic university must be capable of energizing and implementing this kind of program.

D. ACADEMIC FREEDOM

The next topic, academic freedom, is a controversial one and is linked by John Paul II in *Ex Corde Ecclesiae* to the preservation of "the rights of the individual person and of the community . . . within the confines of the truth and the common good" (ECE, I, 12; II, art. 2, 5). Thus, academic freedom in the Catholic university, as university, is to be guaranteed to all its members. Institutional autonomy also is necessary. However, academic freedom (as all freedom) must be distinguished from abuse of freedom, also called license. The basis of this distinction, according to the author, is truth and the common good. Therefore, in exercising academic freedom in the Catholic university, its members must strive to know the truth and to implement the common good. This obviously applies to the faculty in philosophy as well as to faculty in all other disciplines in their teaching and research. While the "audience" for the researcher's publications is somewhat ambiguous, the students in the teacher's classes should be known well enough to allow the norms of academic freedom to be applied in a manner conducive to implementing the goals of the course, the department, the college, and the university. In the teaching and the research, of course, the specific canons and boundaries of each discipline (as philosophy) must be respected.

Behind and beneath this view of academic freedom (and all freedom) is the notion of truth. Freedom without truth is license and is destructive of human well-being. However, according to John Paul II, we must distinguish (as mentioned above) between the ultimate, absolute truth to be known (the proper object of knowledge) and truth as known to human persons (immanent, changing truth). The ultimate, absolute truth in this context is, of course, the Triune God of Christianity, a Personal Being known especially through faith in Jesus Christ, the Second Person of the Blessed Trinity. While this raises further questions about the relationship between philosophy and theology, John Paul II is clear in asserting that "freedom is not expressed in choices made against God. For how can the refusal to be opened up to that which allows . . . complete self-understanding . . . be judged a true use of freedom" (FR, 13)?

The relationship between philosophy and theology in the Catholic university becomes even more complex when the question of implementation in various cultures is raised. Although Christ was born and raised at a specific time and in a specific place, the Church has a mission to "teach all nations," including the possibility of establishing Catholic universities in all nations! Two principles must be considered, according to John Paul II in *Fides et ratio*. First, there is the responsibility to transcend the particular and concrete in order to demonstrate the universality of faith. The unity of the family and children of God must be preserved regardless of the diversity of places and customs. Citing St. Thomas Aquinas (*De Caelo*), John Paul II says that "what matters is 'not what people think, but the nature of truth itself'" (FR, 69). On the other hand, various cultures represent diverse paths to truth and must be respected, and their development must be promoted. While the priority must be given to the truth and the common good as required by a universal human nature, it must be recognized that every freely developing culture will promote this goal. In a Catholic university, achieving this goal means being guided in all phases of institutional endeavors by Scripture, Church Tradition, and the Magisterium. As noted above, however, this kind of theologically-based effort requires philosophical reflection.

E. THE MORAL DIMENSION OF ACADEMIC LIFE

The next major topic, the moral dimension of the Catholic university, while necessitating theology, also involves philosophy as well as a mutual relationship between theology and philosophy. The ethical dimension of the scholarly pursuit of truth in the Catholic university is not overlooked by John Paul II in *Ex Corde Ecclesiae*. In fact, near the outset of the document, he includes as one of the essential features of a Catholic university, *as Catholic*, "an institutional commitment to the service of the people of God and of the human family in their pilgrimage to the transcendent goal which gives meaning to life." (ECE, I, 13). This commitment to ethical activity is aligned with the responsibility of the office of pastoral ministry in the Catholic university to assist its members in "integrating faith with life" (ECE, I, 38), that is, in preparing "for active participation in the life of the Church" (ECE, I, 41). In order to achieve this, to evaluate the values and norms of culture, and to communicate proper ethical/religious principles, a person must *understand* those principles and values through serious studies in philosophical ethics. Such investigations contribute to the teaching and learning as well as to the research in each academic discipline. According to the message of *Ex Corde Ecclesiae*, in the process of Catholic higher education, knowledge must be joined to conscience—always (ECE, I, 18).

What kinds of ethical principles are to permeate the Catholic university? Obviously, the philosophy curriculum must incorporate many different ethical views and systems, including positivistic, atheistic, and other approaches. This is because truth is discovered in many "places"; also, students learn from studying contrasting methods and content. However, somewhere in the philosophy curriculum, students also should study the ethical principles which the Catholic university ought to become known for in its own operation as an academic institution. In general, this means giving priority to the ethical over the technical, to persons over things in the world, to spirit over matter, and most significantly, to God over the human being and all other creation. More specifically, this direction must be appreciated, according to John Paul II in *Fides et ratio* and in *Veritatis splendor*, in terms of the distinction noted above between the objective order of reality transcending time and space, and the human awareness of such truth. Human awareness is never complete and is always changing due to its subjective dimension.

What more can be said to illuminate the nature of this Ultimate Reality, which is the goal of all ethical theory and practice, in accord with John Paul II in *Veritatis splendor*? His answer, not surprisingly, is clear: "People today need to turn to Christ . . . in order to receive from him the answer to their questions about what is good and what is evil. Christ is the Teacher, the Risen One who . . . teaches the truth about moral action" (VS, 8). The author's reason for this position is equally clear: "Only God can answer the questions about what is good, because he is the Good itself" (VS, 9). Therefore, moral action means "following Christ," which entails understanding and conforming internally and externally to one's conscience as guided by the natural law, which is a reflection of eternal law. Formation of conscience (as learning itself) requires a continuous pursuit due to the contingency of the human person and the infinity of the goal sought (VS, 64). It also requires a divine gift because of this discrepancy between the seeker and the sought (VS, 22).

The eternal law or divine law is the "'supreme rule of life . . . the eternal, objective and universal law by which God out of his wisdom and love arranges, directs and governs the whole world and the paths of the human community'" (VS, 43, citing the "Declaration on Religious Freedom" of the Second Vatican Council). Natural law is the "human expression of God's eternal law" or "the participation of the eternal law in the rational creature" (VS, 43). God has implanted this law within us and within the world. It can be known by human reason, but not infallibly. A correct conscience is one which reflects the natural law; it must be formed deliberately through ethical studies and moral activity. While philosophical study ought to be pursued in this connection, it must be complemented by investigations in moral theology, incorporating the study of Scripture, Church Tradition, and the Magisterium. In this regard, John Paul II, in *Veritatis splendor* refers not infrequently to the commandments given to Moses in the Old Covenant and to the Sermon on the Mount. He calls the latter the "magna charta of Gospel morality" because it "contains the fullest and most complete formulation of the new Law" (VS, 12; cf. Matt., 5–7).

Another requisite for knowing the truth and living a good Christian life is freedom. The author of *Veritatis splendor* says that "there can be no morality without freedom . . . " (VS, 34). Freedom to him means more than a choice among particular actions; it is "*a decision about oneself* and a setting of one's own life for or against the Good, for or against the Truth, and ultimately for or against God" (VS, 65). Therefore, obedience to the natural law—which is obedience to God—does not interfere with one's freedom. Rather, living in accord with God's law (eternal law reflected in natural law) is equivalent to living a good life, which means freely living in accord with one's true nature (VS, 40). Therefore, according to John Paul II, the authentic moral life is Christ-centered, thus God-centered. What ought the Catholic university to do in promoting this kind of living? While it is obvious that knowing the truth does not guarantee living the good life, the study of moral philosophy in the Catholic university must be required of all students simply because of the goals of the university and the fact that one cannot do what is good in a genuinely human manner without knowing the truth. Therefore, the academic learning is essential and should be augmented, according to John Paul II, by the campus ministry programs, which promote the application of truth to living a good Christian life.

F. THE ACADEMIC COMMUNITY

The next topic to be considered in accord with the thought of John Paul II in these three official Church documents is the university community. What ought to characterize this community of learners, including researchers, teachers and students? According to John Paul II in *Ex Corde Ecclesiae*, the inspiration for everyone in this academic community in all activities is the truth, and the key to the truth is the "spirit of Christ," the basis for recognizing the dignity of the human person. The search for truth should be ingrained in each member of the community as a lifelong endeavor. "Animated by a spirit of freedom and charity" (ECE, I, 21), this community should combine humanistic and cultural development with liberal, technical, and professional learning. The core of the community life, love of God and of neighbor, involves knowledge, attitude, and action directed freely to the service of other persons for the sake of the love of God (VS, 20). The source and example *par excellence* of such love is Christ crucified, Whose "way of acting . . . his words, his deeds, and his precepts constitute the moral rule of Christian life" (VS, 20). This is the kind of love which should inspire the united search for truth and meaning, and the united efforts to communicate that truth and meaning—"united" in the sense of cooperation rather than competition, which means all assisting all with the intent of enabling everyone to *do* better and to *be* better in terms of personal potential.

The role of belief in all human knowledge and of trust in terrestrial pursuits of truth underscores the communal feature of research, teaching, and learning in the Catholic university, according to John Paul II in *Fides et ratio*. He says that while believing is a less perfect form of awareness than that of personal recognition, it "seems richer than mere evidence" "because it brings with it an interpersonal relationship and activates . . . [a] profound capacity for trusting other persons and . . . establishing a stronger and more intimate relationship with them," thereby promoting "a living habit of self-giving and fidelity towards others" (FR, 32). The author of *Fides et ratio* asserts that "the capacity for committing oneself and one's life to another person, anthropologically speaking, are among the most significant and expressive of human acts" (FR, 33). What does this mean for the philosophy faculty and students in a Catholic university? One is reminded of the friendship that became an important ingredient for sound philosophizing according to Plato and Aristotle. In more practical terms, this signifies the need for cooperation among faculty members in their research and in their teaching, cooperation among students in assisting one another to learn, and an awareness of students' difficulties on the part of the faculty in assisting students to learn.

These principles of John Paul II also call for friendly cooperation between the departments of philosophy and theology. There may even be team teaching which engages the two units as well as cross-listed courses such as in areas of philosophical theology and philosophy of religion. The principles of many great thinkers such as Augustine and St. Thomas Aquinas might be taught in both philosophy and theology. In any case, the whole idea of "Christian philosophy" must permeate the research and teaching of philosophy in a Catholic university which is responding to the call of John Paul II for such an institution in conjunction with the Catholic Church.

G. HUMAN NATURE

Mentioned last among the topics considered in analyzing John Paul II's view of the Catholic university in *Ex Corde Ecclesiae* (1990), in conjunction with *Veritatis splendor* (1993) and *Fides et ratio* (1998), and related to all of them is the meaning of "human nature." What it means to be a human being is crucial to every plan of education and to the continuing effort to implement that plan. This issue is inextricably linked, of course, to the notion of truth in both its objective, transcendent meaning (truth to be known) and its subjective, immanent meaning (truth as known). What does John Paul II say about the nature of the human person in these three documents? First of all, there is a God-given human nature shared by all human persons. Every human being, while accidentally different from all other human beings, possesses the same essence as every other human being. But, what is that essence? What is common to all humans? Answering this question is a major desideratum of a Catholic university, according to the author of *Ex Corde Ecclesiae* (ECE, I, 33). This means the inclusion of a course in philosophical anthropology, including the Christian dimension of the discipline, in the philosophy curriculum.

While (John Paul II says) empirical methods and behavioral sciences provide valuable data about human living, they cannot provide a full explanation of human nature because every human being possesses an inseparable unity of body and soul (VS, 49). Furthermore, self-realization requires following Christ in living an authentic moral life—which demands divine faith as well as reason, along with the help of God (VS, 14, 20). The call of God to love God and to love one's neighbor as oneself seeks a free response. All this defies evidence provided by empiricists, positivists, and other radical relativists. Also, the BIG questions of life, those which *all* human beings ask and which betray a human need for an absolute being, a final explanation, and a supreme value cannot be addressed through radical relativism by the very nature of such thought. Again, this Christian view of human nature, while inviting the study of empiricist and related philosophies, requires the study of philosophies "open to transcendence" as well as the study of relationships between philosophy and theology, including Catholic theology.

NOTES

1. In this section of the paper, references to these three documents will be indicated in parentheses within the text by the following abbreviations: ECE (*Ex Corde Ecclesiae*), VS (*Veritatis splendor*), and FR (*Fides et ratio*).

2. Robert Sokolowski, "The Autonomy of Philosophy," *Fides et ratio, Restoring Faith in Reason*, Eds. T.B. Hemming and S.F. Parsons (Notre Dame, IN: University of Norte Dame Press 2003), 277–91.

Conclusion

In these two chapters I have surveyed selected aspects of twentieth-century philosophy in the United States and principles of Pope John Paul II pertaining to the ideal of a Catholic university, claiming that applying the latter to American Catholic universities can contribute to counteracting negative effects of the direction instigated by twentieth-century American philosophy. The central question remaining to be considered, therefore, is *how* John Paul II's principles address the current cultural crisis which so many associate with mainstream American philosophy in the twentieth century. First of all, how can we summarize this crisis of values? Secondly, what features of John Paul II's three documents pertain to the rectification of cultural issues in the US — and what reasons can be adduced to support the claim of amelioration?

Before confronting these central issues, I wish to say a few words about the viewpoint and criteria employed in the selection of principles in Chapter One, in judging that there is a cultural crisis, and in claiming that applying principles of John Paul II (in Chapter Two) can alleviate this crisis of values. The cultural crisis associated with the history of twentieth-century philosophy in the United States has been analyzed here from a viewpoint compatible with Christianity — but not only Christianity. Perhaps, the simplest way to explain this intellectual posture in terms of its lowest common denominator is to raise two (oversimplified) questions. 1) Is there some ultimate reality (that is, beyond space and time) which serves as a criterion for judging good and evil, the proper direction of one's life, etc.? 2) Or, do all things (at least, knowable things) constantly change, rendering good and evil, and all value judgments, radically relative? The ultimate reality referred in question #1 could be an abstract principle, such as the Good of Plato or the First Cause of Aristotle. However, it also could be a Personal Being to whom human beings can relate, as in Christianity, Islam, and Judaism. In any case, human knowledge is always subjective and relative because the faculty of judgment is finite and inherent in a changing being. However, the object of knowledge (the knowable) varies dramatically in questions #1 and #2 above. In #1 the object of knowledge is understood (believed) to be permanent, thereby providing a direction for human living and a criterion or measure for distinguishing good and evil. In #2 the object of knowledge is constantly changing. Therefore, the human person maintaining this stance faces a situation which can be described as "radically relative." In these circumstances, there are no guidelines for human living outside of the natural process of life itself. This means that, strictly speaking, one should exhibit an indifference to any questions or search directed beyond the natural, continuing process of life as it has been and is being experienced among human beings.

This second alternative, pertaining to the radically relative, is seen here to characterize the general direction—and the result—of the history of mainstream American philosophy in the twentieth century. The antidote proposed in terms of principles of John Paul II obviously represents not merely a Platonic or Aristotelian vision, but a Catholic Christian stance. (It should be noted, however, that critics of the radically relative features of American culture have much in common despite fundamental differences concerning the nature of an Ultimate Reality.) In any case, from a Christian viewpoint (adopted here), the negative effects of the general direction of mainstream American philosophy in the twentieth century are seen to be most unfortunate in regard to what is denied: the intelligibility of any transcendent, ultimate reality; the meaningfulness of *questions* pertaining to such a being; and (eventually) the usefulness of reason itself. The obvious direction of these denials in regard to philosophy itself is the narrowing of its scope from the BIG questions of life, those which human beings by nature inevitably continue to ask, to questions concerning specific, concrete (past or present) situations, to questions concerning the meaning of language, to a relegation of all questions to the social sciences—in case any meaning is still possible! In other words, philosophy has become bankrupt; it has no audience because it has no content.

While it might be possible to hold this view of philosophy and simultaneously to adhere to some kind of supernatural faith, that is not what has been happening recently in the United States. Early in the twentieth century mainstream American philosophy rejected any possibility of a relationship to theology, especially Christian modes of theology. This was a response, of course, consistent with the narrowing scope of philosophy. Furthermore, a Christian theology devoid of reason is an impossibility anyway. What many apparently have failed to detect is that narrowing the scope of philosophy narrows the scope of human freedom. Eliminating theology extends this limitation of human freedom. There is no longer (in this kind of situation) any possibility of rational reflection or disputation in decision-making—there is no basis for it. The only appeal for individuals is to feeling, to "what works" (hopefully!), or to "what everyone is saying or doing." The only appeal for groups is to power.

What is there in the principles of Pope John Paul II that can possibly address this cultural vacuum if implemented in the teaching of philosophy in Catholic universities in the United States? First of all, John Paul II recognizes as essential and central to philosophy the kinds of *questions* that human persons by nature inevitably ask in seeking meaning and happiness in their lives. These questions include the familiar ones: What is my most original source? Why am I here? What is my ultimate destination? What are the differences between good and evil? How is truth to be distinguished from falsehood? What makes me truly free and happy? These kinds of questions and the kinds of philosophy in which they are embedded must be integral to the curriculum of American Catholic universities. This means, of course, that *all* students must be exposed to these kinds of philosophy—which does not mean that the curriculum should be restricted to only these kinds of philosophy.

Secondly, John Paul II distinguishes clearly between a transcendent, permanent object of knowledge, which must be sought continuously through the study of philosophy. This does not mean that pragmatism, empiricism, naturalism, etc. should not be taught, but it does mean that exclusive attention to philosophies immersed in radical relativism is inappropriate because it is destructive of authentic human learning. The continuous search for this ultimate reality must characterize the whole American Catholic university community, of course. If the philosophy faculty is not continuing to learn (including their public learning in the process of teaching), students will not continue to learn either. The kinds of philosophy proposed by John Paul II are focused upon the kinds of questions which are fascinating and intriguing because they address truly human issues.

Thirdly, the search proposed by John Paul II embodies not only questions, but also answers. In fact, he would say that without some answers, it becomes impossible to raise meaningful questions, and to find direction and meaning in life. A key to discovering answers, which can be known at least partially, lies in his proposed dialogue between faith and reason. While philosophy alone can achieve the truth to some extent and is a legitimate enterprise in itself, it falls short of fulfillment unless it is conjoined in a proper manner with divine faith and Catholic theology. For American Catholic universities, this means teaching (truly teaching, as distinct from indoctrinating) theology to all students. It means teaching non-Catholic and non-Christian religions as well, but not exclusively. This union between philosophy and theology can be implemented in American Catholic universities in various manners. A prime example would be courses in Christian philosophy and philosophy of religion. Other examples would include team teaching between faculty of the philosophy and theology departments, interdepartmental seminars, and symposia featuring philosophical and theological dimensions of the same topic.

Fourthly, united with the teaching of Catholic theology within American Catholic universities, Pope John Paul II recommends that the entire academic community, inspired by Jesus Christ, who is God, provide meaningful service to the "people of God." This pertains to the moral dimension of these institutions and to the integration of faith with life. This academic community, according to John Paul II, will know not only what kind of service to render to others, but also *why* it ought to be done. The model, of course, is the life of Christ. This dimension, while directly related to and flowing from the teaching of philosophy and theology, can be organized and overseen by campus ministry personnel.

In conclusion to this effort to relate the principles of John Paul II to the current cultural vacuum in the United States, we must notice that the significance of faith is inestimable. This includes natural or philosophical faith, which represents an integral dimension of *all* that is said to be "known," but it means to the author of the three papal documents analyzed above especially divine faith, which requires the grace of God. This kind of faith is required to know the Jesus of history and the Triune God of Christianity. However, faith is also demanded for recognizing and searching for (the recognition is required for the searching) a Platonic World of Ideas. In fact, some kind of faith is requisite to restricting one's vision to the natural world. We must notice how these different kinds and directions of faith lead to different kinds of searches for reality and different kinds of conclusions. In American Catholic universities inspired by the principles of John Paul II, faith will be united with reason, and theology with philosophy in a continuous search for the God Who has created us, Who loves us, and Who has redeemed us.

Instead of narrowing the students' vision, teaching in this kind of context in American Catholic universities will expand their vision; instead of stifling their interest, it will enhance their interest; instead of restricting their freedom, it will increase their freedom; instead of diminishing conversation and community, it will embellish them; instead of discouraging service to others, it will encourage such service.

Bibliography of Materials Used

Barrett, William, and Henry D. Aiken (eds.). *Philosophy in the Twentieth Century: An Anthology.* Vol. I. New York: Random House, 1962. See essay by Aiken, "The Fate of Philosophy in the Twentieth Century."

Bertocci, Peter (ed.). *Mid-Twentieth Century American Philosophy: Personal Statements.* New York: Humanities Press, 1974. See "Preface" by Bertocci, and essay by Paul Weiss, "The Philosophic Quest."

Bowers, David F. (ed.). *Foreign Influences in American Life: Essays and Critical Bibliographies.* New York: Peter Smith, 1952. See Bower's essay, "Hegel, Darwin, and the American Tradition."

Cahoone, Lawrence (ed.). *From Modernism to Postmodernism: An Anthology.* Expanded second edition. Oxford: Blackwell Publishing, 2003. See "Introduction" by Cahoone.

Chase, J.W. (ed.). *Years of the Modern: An American Appraisal.* New York: Longmans, Green and Company, 1949. See essay by Henry Steele Commager, "Portrait of the American."

Commager, Henry Steele. *The American Mind: An Interpretation of American Thought and Character Since the 1880's.* New Haven, CT: Yale University Press, 1950.

Connor, Steven (ed.). *The Cambridge Companion to Postmodernism.* Cambridge: University Press, 2004. See "Introduction" by Connor.

Copleston, Frederick, S.J. *Contemporary Philosophy: Studies of Logical Positivism and Existentiatism.* Paramus, NJ, and New York: Newman Press, 1966.

De Lubac, Henri, S.J. *The Drama of Atheist Humanism.* Tr. Edith M. Riley. Cleveland and New York: Meridian Books, 1963; New York: Sheed and Waud, Inc., 1950.

Dewey, John. *The Influence of Darwin on Philosophy: and Other Essays in Contemporary Thought.* New York: Peter Smith, 1951; Henry Holt and Company, 1910.

Easton, Loyd D. *Hegel's First American Followers, the Ohio Hegelians: J. G. Stallo, Peter Kaufman, Moncure Conway, August Willich.* Athens, OH: Ohio University Press, 1966.

Goetzmann, William H. (ed.). *The American Hegelians: An Intellectual Episode in the History of Western America*. New York: Alfred A. Knopf, 1973.
Harmon, Francis B. *The Social Philosophy of the St. Louis Hegelians*. New York: Columbia University Press, 1943.
John Paul II, Pope. *Ex Corde Ecclesiae*. Apostolic Constitution, promulgated in 1990.
——. *Fides et ratio*. Encyclical Letter, 1998.
——. *Veritatis splendor*. Encyclical Letter, 1993.
Koch, Adrienne. *The Philosophy of Thomas Jefferson*. Chicago: Quadrangle Books, University of Chicago Press, 1964.
Kuklick, Bruce. *The Rise of American Philosophy: Cambridge, Massachusetts, 1860-1930*. New Haven, CT, and London: Yale University Press, 1977.
Kurtz, Paul (ed.). *American Philosophy in the Twentieth Century: A Sourcebook from Pragmatism to Philosophical Analysis*. New York: The Macmillan Company; London: Collier-Macmillan, Ltd., 1966.
——. (ed.). *American Thought Before 1900: A Sourcebook from Puritanism to Darwinism*. New York: The Macmillan Company; London: Collier-Macmillan, Ltd., 1966.
Macquarrie, John. *Twentieth-Century Religious Thought: The Frontiers of Philosophy and Theology, 1900-1970*. Revised edition. London: SCM Press, Ltd., 1971.
Marsden, George M. *The Outrageous Idea of Christian Scholarship*. Oxford, New York: Oxford University Press, 1997.
——. *The Soul of the American University: From Protestant Establishment to Established Nonbelief*. New York: Oxford University Press, 1994.
Marsden, George M., and Bradley J. Longfield (eds.). *The Secularization of the Academy*. New York and Oxford: Oxford University Press, 1992.
Perry, Charles M. *The St. Louis Movement in Philosophy*. Norman, OK: University of Oklahoma Press, 1930.
Pochmann, Henry A. *German Culture in America*. Madison, WI: University of Wisconsin Press, 1957.
——. (ed.). *New England Transcendentalism and St. Louis Hegelianism*. Philadelphia: Carl Schurz Memorial Foundation, 1948.
Schall, James V., S.J. *The Regensburg Lecture*. South Bend, IN: St. Augustine's Press, 2007.
Smith, John E. *The Spirit of American Philosophy*. Revised edition. Albany: State University of New York Press, 1983.
Snider, Denton J. *The St. Louis Movement in Philosophy*. St. Louis: Sigma Publishing Company, 1920.
Sokolowski, Robert. "The Autonomy of Philosophy," *Fides et ratio, Restoring Faith in Reason*. Eds. T.B. Hemming and S.F. Parsons. Notre Dame, IN: University of Notre Dame Press, 2002.
Werkmeister, W.H. *A History of Philosophical Ideas in America*. New York: The Ronald Press Company, 1949.
Woods, Thomas B. "None So Blind: How Secularists Ignore the Value of Religion" *Crisis: Politics, Culture, and the Church*, 23 (November, 2005).

Index

"age of anxiety," 21
Aiken, Henry D., 20
American Catholic universities, vii, viii, xii, 41, 43, 44
American intellectual history, 12
American intellectual revolution, 10
American (U.S.) philosophy, 6, 9, 10, 11, 14, 19, 21, 22, 28n115, 42
analytic philosophy, 1, 12, 13, 20
Aquinas, St. Thomas, 14, 34 (cited by Pope John Paul II)
Aristotle, 30, 37, 41
Augustine, St. Aureluis, 38
Austin, John, 13

"beyond agnosticism," vii, 10, 12, 14, 20, 28n115
"beyond relativism," 18, 21
bifurcation of fact and reason, 15
BIG questions of life, 42
Black, Max, 13
black theology, 17
Bouwsma, O.K., 13
Bowne, Borden Parker, 5
Bridgman, P.W., 26n76
Brockmeyer, Henry C., 5, 22n5

Carnap, Rudolf, 13
Catholic Church, 22

Catholic higher education, 19
Catholic liberal arts college, xi
Center for Process Studies, 28n116
Christian theology, 42
Christianity, 21, 22, 30, 41
Commager, Henry Steele, 8, 10
"common faith," 3, 4
Comte, Auguste, 25n63
crisis of values, 41
"Critical Realists," 7
cultural crisis, 41
cultural revolution, 2, 4, 5, 9, 10
cultural vacuum, 43, 44

Darwin, Charles, 2, 4, 5, 23n21
Darwinism, 5, 23n18
"Death of God," 17
"deconstruction," 18
Deism, 1
Deleuze, Gilles, 17
Derrida, Jacques, 17
de Saussure, Ferdinand, 17
Descartes, René, 24n25
determinism, 13
Dewey, John, vii, 5, 7, 9, 10, 12, 20, 24n24, 25n49, 28n115
"Dionysian religion," 17
dualism, 13

Edwards, Jonathan, 1
empiricism, 4, 9, 10, 43
empiricists, 38
Enlightenment, 17
epistemology, 11, 18, 19, 20, 28n116
ethics (or moral philosophy), 20, 26–27n89
existentialism, 1, 15, 16, 17

Feigl, Herbert, 12
Foucault, Michel, 17
Franklin, Benjamin, 1
"frontier(s) of (between) theology and philosophy," 15, 16, 19

God, 10, 19, 21; Absolute, 13; Absolute Being, 7; Transcendent Being, or transcendent being, 10, 12; Ultimate Reality, 42
"Golden Age of American Philosophy, vii, 7
Goodman, Nelson, 13

Harris, William Torrey, 1, 5, 22n5
Hegel, G.F.W., 4, 5, 23n21, 23n22
Hegelian—Darwinian synthesis, 5
Hegelianism, 5, 23n18
Hempel, Carl, 12
history of philosophy, 22
Howison, George H., 5
human freedom, 43

idealism, 1, 2, 5, 6, 7, 10, 15, 19, 22n5, 27n92; critical (neo-Kantian) idealism, 27n92; speculative (neo-Hegelian) idealism, 27n92; absolute idealism, 27n92; personal idealism, 27n92
"immanence of norms," 18
instrumentalism, 5, 9
Irigaray, Luce, 17
Islam, 30, 41

Jakobson, Roman, 17
James, William, 6, 7, 10, 12

Jefferson, Thomas, 1, 9, 10, 12
John Paul II (pope), viii, xii, 22, 29, 30, 31, 32, 33, 34, 35, 36, 37, 38, 39, 42, 43, 44; academic discipline(s), 31, 35; academic freedom, 33, 34; behavioral sciences, 38; campus ministry programs, 36; Catholic theology, 39, 43, 44; Catholic university, xii, 22, 29, 30, 31, 32, 33, 34, 35, 36, 37, 38, 41; Christ: the center of creation and of human history, 31; crucified, 37; as model of moral life, 38, 44; the Risen One, 35; the Teacher, 35; "Christian philosophy," 38, 44; "circle of the arts and sciences," 31; common good, 34; conscience, 35, 36; curriculum, 31; philosophy, 35; "Declaration on Religious Freedom" (Vatican II), 36; divine faith, 44; empirical methods, 38; eternal (divine) law, 35, 36; eternal expressions of truth, 30; eternal truths, 30; *Ex Corde Ecclesiae* (1990), viii, xii, 29, 30, 31, 32, 33, 35, 37, 38, 39n1; faith (or belief): natural, 32; and reason, 30, 32, 33, 43; role in all human knowledge, 37; supernatural, 32; *Fides et ratio* (1998), viii, xii, 29, 31, 32, 33, 34, 35, 37, 38, 39n1; first principles, 31, 32; freedom in relationship to morality, 36; God: absolute being, 38; as achieved in philosophy, 43; Creator of the World, 3; the Good, 35; in His everlasting glory, 30; as inspiration of meaningful service to others, 44; and moral action, 35; "object" of faith and knowledge, 33; "object" of human love, 37; "object" of human search, 37; "object" of supernatural faith, 32; One, 31; Personal Being, 34, 41; in relationship to human freedom, 34; in relationship to a

"good Christian life," 36; source of all things, 34; as transcendent, 39; Triune, 34, 44; Ultimate Reality, 35, 41; Who is Truth, 30; human nature: as universal, 34; integration of faith with life, 44; integration of knowledge, 31; Jesus Christ, who is God, xii; Second Person of the Blessed Trinity, 34; license, as abuse of freedom, 33; magisterium, 34, 36; meaning, 29, 30, 43; moral philosophy, 36; moral rule of Christian life, 37; natural law, 35, 36; objects of knowledge, 31; philosophical ethics, 35; philosophical realism, 11; philosophy in Catholic higher education, 19, 43; philosophy and theology (and vice versa), 31, 34, 35, 38, 39, 43, 44; Roman Catholic Church, xii, 29; Scripture, 34, 36; search, 29, 30; Second Vatican Council, 36; Sermon on the Mount, 36; Tradition (Church), 34, 36; transcendence, 32; truth: achieved in philosophy, 43; concerning moral action, 35; focal point of a Catholic university, 29; fount of, 30; object of human search, 37; objective, 31; oneness of, 31; relationship to freedom, 34; relationship to a "good Christian life," 36; the search for, 30; source of distinction between freedom and license, 33; whole, 31; *Veritatis splendor* (1993), viii, xii, 29, 35, 36, 38, 39n1
Journal of Speculative Philosophy, 22n5
Judaism, 30, 41

kerygmatic theology, 1

Levi-Strauss, Claude, 17
Lewis, C.I., 20, 25n43, 26n76
linguistic analysis, vii, 11, 12, 13, 21
"linguistic turn" of philosophy, 14

linguistics, 21
logic, 11, 13, 19, 20
logical empiricism, 21
logical positivism, vii, 11, 12, 13, 16
Lovejoy, Arthur O., 7
Lyotard, Jean-Francois, 17

Macquarrie, John, 15
Mann, Horace, 1, 12
Marxism, 1, 15
materialism, 1, 28n116
Merleau-Ponty, Maurice, 17
"meta-ethics," 21
Metaphysical Club, 1
metaphysics, vii, 6, 7, 13, 16, 20, 27n97
Mind and World Order (1929), 20, 25n43
Montagne, William P., 7
Montessori, Maria, 12
Moore, G.E., 12, 13, 16
mystical philosophy, 11

naturalism, vii, xi, 1, 2, 6, 7, 9, 11, 19, 43
nature, 19, 21
neo-empiricism, vii, 14
neo-scholasticism, 16
neo-Thomism, 15, 16
"new hermeneutics," 17
"new realism," 11, 16
"New Realists," 7
Nietzsche, Friedrich, 17

Origin of Species (1859), 2, 4

Peirce, Charles, 1, 6, 7, 10, 12
Perry, Ralph Barton, 7
phenomenology, 1, 15, 17
philosophical (natural) faith, 44
philosophical revolution, 8, 9, 19
philosophical theology, 27n91, 38
philosophy of education, 28n115
philosophy of religion, 8, 27n91, 28n116, 38, 44
Plato, 30, 31, 37, 41

Platonic World of Ideas, 44
positivism, 1, 9, 12
positivists, 38
postmodernism (postmodernists), vii, 1, 17, 18, 20
postmodernist movement. *See* postmodernism
"post-structuralists," 18
pragmatism, vii, xi, 1, 6, 11, 12, 19, 43
professionalization of philosophy, 8, 11, 21
Protestant Reformation, 10
Puritanism, 1

Quine, W.V., 13

radical relativism, 38, 43
radically relative, 41, 42
realism, vii, xi, 1, 6, 7, 9, 11, 19
realist metaphysics, 16
reason, 19, 21
Reichenbach, Hans, 12
relativism, 17, 19
religion, 9, 13, 26–27n89
religious philosophy (or philosophies), 8, 19
Royce, Josiah, 6, 7
Russell, Bertrand, 12, 13, 16
Ryle, Gilbert, 13

Santayana, George, 7
Sartre, Jean-Paul, 17
Schlick, Moritz, 12

scientism, 8, 9, 10
Scotus, Duns, 14
secularization, 8, 10, 21
Smith, John E., 14, 26–27n89
social sciences, 28n115
Socrates, 30
speculative philosophy, 13
Spencer, Herbert, 4
St. Louis Hegelians, 22n5
structuralism, 17
supernatural faith, 42
synoptic worldviews, 19

Tarski, Alfred, 12
"theology of hope," 17
Thomism, 1
transcendental Thomism, 17
Transcendentalism, 1, 2, 5, 22n5
truth (postmodernist view of), 18
Tufts, James H., 10

ultimate reality, 43
Unitarianism, 1

Verifiability Principle, 13
Vienna Circle, 26n74

"watershed," 2, 15
Weiss, Paul, 14
Whitehead, A.N., 7, 15
Wittgenstein, Ludwig, 12, 13, 26n74

Zen Buddhism, 1

About the Author

The author earned a B.A. degree in philosophy from Loras College, Dubuque, Iowa; and M.A. and Ph.D degrees in philosophy of education from the Catholic University of America, Washington D.C. He has taught in schools and departments of philosophy, and schools and departments of education, He taught for thirty-two years at Marquette University, Milwaukee, Wisconsin; and has taught in other universities in the United States (including the island of Guam), the Philippines, Thailand and Taiwan. His articles in philosophy and education have appeared in about thirty different scholarly journals published in the United States, Australia, England, Ireland, India and the Philippines. His book on the philosophy of education of William Torrey Harris also was published by the University Press of America. He currently is a Senior Research Associate at the Institute for History of Philosophy and Pedagogy in Rockville, Maryland.

www.ingramcontent.com/pod-product-compliance
Lightning Source LLC
Chambersburg PA
CBHW031555300426
44111CB00006BA/328